Properties of Crystals, Gems, Stones, Shells & Metals

By: Kristina Benson

The Complete Reference to Magickal Gems, Stones, Shells and Metals

ISBN 13: 978-1-60332-020-7

Printed in the United States of America

Table of contents

INTRODUCTION.. 4
How to use this book... 5

BASIC CRYSTAL SELECTION & CARE 7
Charging and Cleansing Your Crystals 7
Bathing.. 8
Burying... 9

GEMS, STONES, AND CRYSTALS...................................... 11
A...12
B.. 29
C.. 33
D..48
E.. 52
F.. 55
G..57
H..61
I... 64
J... 65
K..71
L... 74
M 78
N..86
O... 87
P 93
Q... 100
R 106
S 112
T 128
U..134
V..136
W..137
Z 138

INTRODUCTION

This book is intended for those who are familiar with the benefits of using crystals in meditation, chakra work, reiki, yoga, and spells. I have included, however, a brief description of basic crystal selection and care for those who are just beginning to develop an interest in the art of crystals.

It should be noted that the word "stone" and "crystal", when used herewith, are not used to indicate precise scientific meanings. A "stone", in geological lexicon, is a piece of rock, while a "crystal" is a solid in which its atoms, molecules, or ions are stacked in a regularly ordered, repeating pattern extending in all three spatial dimensions. "Gems" are essentially a word for minerals that are cut in a specific way, or have a significant monetary value. I use the words stone, crystal, and gem very loosely, and strict adherence to geological lexicon shouldn't be assumed here.

How to use this book

The stones are listed in alphabetical order, and I've discussed their benefits in chakra work, meditation, and occasionally reiki and feng shui. There is an index in the back so that you can look up a specific ailment or concern that you might have, and find the best crystal to help cure or soothe your particular affliction.

As always, however, use common sense. If you suspect that you have an illness or disorder, don't use this information as a substitute for your doctor or wellness practitioner.

That said, we'll move on to a short section on crystal selection and care.

BASIC CRYSTAL SELECTION & CARE

Crystals can be chosen to aid in specific healing and meditative practices. When it comes to selecting the crystals you will work with, I would recommend that you go to a store that will allow you to not only look at, but touch them. You will find that the right crystal will identify itself quickly. Though there are many reputable online stores that sell crystals, it is difficult to assess their individual energies and vibrations without touching and holding them.

While perusing gems and crystals you may find that a particular item draws you to it. Follow your instincts. Your body and psyche needs all 7 colors: red, orange, yellow, green, blue, indigo and violet and you may unconsciously be drawn to the gems or crystals that are most appropriate for you.

Charging & Cleansing Your Crystals

Before you start to use your crystals you should clean and charge them to remove any negative energy or vibrations from others who may have handled them. There are several easy ways to cleanse your crystals:

Bathing

Soak your crystal in one cup of sea salt dissolved in one quart of purified or spring water. Use a glass or porcelain bowl as silver or copper may interfere with the crystals' natural vibrations. When you place them in the bowl, meditate on them and ask that they are cleared. Leave them for at least an hour but they can soak for a day without harm.

Sunshine Bath

Place your crystal in direct sunlight for at least four hours. When you place each crystal, meditate and ask that the crystal is cleared.

Moonlight Bath

Place your crystal in the light of a full moon for at least four ours. When you place each crystal, meditate and ask that the crystal is cleared.

Burying

Wrap your crystal in cotton, silk or linen and bury it in a place you feel comfortable for at least 24 hours.

After you have used one or more of these methods, they are ready to be charged. To charge your crystal, hold it while you meditate in order to infuse it with good, healing energy. Some crystals and stones are better at absorbing energy than others, but this is still an important step!

After your crystal has been charged, it is ready for use in reiki, meditation, gazing, gem layouts, feng shui, or whatever you desire.

GEMS, STONES, & CRYSTALS

A

Abalone:

Abalones are marine snails, and are part of the large class Gastropoda, and are usually found off the coasts of S. America, Japan, and China. Ground abalone shell supplements are sometimes taken by athletes to help build and maintain muscle tissue, as the shell of the abalone is known for being exceptionally strong. The abalone's flattened; oval shape with iridescent interior was used by the Native Northwest American Indians in rituals and prayer. Using an abalone in your own rituals, prayers, and spells. A very popular use for abalone is for empowering love spells and talismans. Wearing abalone shell as an amulet will protect the wearer from negativity, both internal and external. The abalone amulet should be charged with a protection spell before use.

Agate:

The appearance of the stone is waxy, smooth, and soft, sometimes with concentric rings of varying colors. Agate will focus your concentration during a ritual, and if carried as a talisman, will help achieve emotional balance, and raise consciousness. Can also be used in chakra work to bring energy to the stomach, colon, liver, spleen, kidneys.

Reduces tension, dampens pain and releases fear, and in general, is great to gaze into when engaging in meditative work. Its properties are subtle but powerful, and work slowly but surely.

Black/Banded Agate:

This stone is especially useful grounding and centering the energies of the Root or Base Chakra. It can be used in meditation, or rituals seeking to heal emotional scars or calm anxiety. The stone channels earth energy, and is an excellent addition to any spell or talisman seeking to bring calm, peace, or stability.

Blue Lace:

Heals wounds both physical and emotional, and although it is of the earth, contains some air elements. Works especially well on the Heart chakra. Strengthens hereditary skeletal structure, outward manifested growths, Arthritis. This is a calming stone, and can be used for meditation, or in rituals to ease emotional scarring or pain. It can also help with self control, grounding, and anxiety.

Botswana Agate:

Gray and waxy in appearance. Helps cope with heat, smoke, and smog. Helpful for anyone who wants to quit smoking and counters some of the unpleasant side effects of smoking by increasing circulation to the skin. This is a particularly useful stone for dealing with change of any kind. Gentle and comforting, it acts as a balm when dealing with stress and uncertainty. Botswana Agate can also help those who are agoraphobic or suffering from social anxiety, offering comfort and protection, especially in crowds.

Fire Agate:

Comes in shades of orange, brown, blue, or green. Strong connection to the energies of the earth. Excellent stone to use before meditating. Fire Agate has a deep calming energy that brings security and safety. Like most agates, it is a protection stone with strong centering powers. Though of the earth, fire agate links to the fire element and can open the base chakra, stimulating sexual energy and acting as an aphrodisiac. Also can act to soothe anxiety in periods of especially acute transition.

Moss Agate:

Connects strongly to the Earth energies, and acts to bind one to Nature and connect with primal rhythms of the earth. Improves ego and self-esteem, increases ability to synchronize and harmonize with environment, and relieves exhaustion.

Plum (Purple) Agate:

This is a stone of meditation and spiritual transformation and can strongly enhance any chakra work with the third eye chakra. Plum agate is a meditation, astral projection, and divination aid. This stone also helps the wearer or holder get in touch with his or her intuition and inner self. Can raise consciousness of surrounding vibrations, and lend stability and calm to spiritual pursuits.

Red/Banded Agate:

This is a great stone for grounding and centering the energies of the Root Chakra, and helps with self confidence and inner conviction. Can help the wearer or bearer get in touch with physical strength and endurance. Also aids in healing physical wounds, and helps with imbalances and diseases of the blood. Good addition to protection charms or spells.

Albite:

White translucent stone with a bluish tinge. Albite
encourages communication and positive exchanges of
energy. Relieves stress and depression and can be used as a
booster for the immune and respiratory systems, as well as
the spleen.

Alexandrite:

Clear violet-green, this powerful and rare stone works to
center, boost self esteem, open the bearer to surrounding
vibrations, and allow the closed-hearted to experience love
and joy. Is particularly useful for chakra work and massage
involving the Heart and Third Eye. Can also assist in
calming nerves, and nervous disorders.

Amazonite:

This stone increases and channels all forms of prosperity,
while at the same time diffusing and reflecting negative
energy and vibrations. Particularly good for chakra work
with the throat, heart, and solar plexus. Creates a feeling of
power, restores spiritual faith and stamina, and soothes
and calms the wearer/bearer as well as all who come in

contact with him/her. Opens channels for communication, inspires trust in others, and helps foster inner convictions, confidence and charisma. As it aids in communication, it is a great stone for writers, singers, or other artists to carry for inspiration in work.

Amber:

Clear yellow or orange, amber is actually not a stone; it is made of petrified, ancient resin and has electromagnetic properties. Opens solar plexus chakra and lends to mental acuity, self confidence, and clear thinking. Also helps with stomach problems, anxiety, issues with the spine, problems with the central nervous system, and memory loss. Excellent for boosting physical and emotional detoxification ceremonies, diets, and rituals. Draws disease out of afflicted areas and neutralizes negative energy. It is a grounding substance with a lot of earth energy. Acts as a magnet to draw negative energy from the room or the bearer. Can help with dream recall, and with remembering past lives. Can relieve headache, hasten and ease childbirth, and reduce fever. Is primarily useful when working with the second Chakra.

Amethyst:

Brings calmness and clarity, and is a wonderful stone when working in times of confusion or chaos. Provides common sense and flexibility in times of crisis. Strengthens and enhances psychic abilities, and ability to tune in with external vibrations and energies. Can help reduce nightmares at night and anxiety during the day. Most effective on the Crown Chakra. Amethyst is considered an excellent healing stone because of its abilities to allow the bearer to self-soothe and find strength in chaos. This crystal is the most recommended stone for stress relief. In addition to assisting with matters of the psyche, it strengthens the cleansing organs and the circulatory system. Helps break free from addictions, including those to food, sex, and unhealthy behavioral patterns. Boosts the memory and motivation to stay sober, or goal oriented. Can benefit people with insomnia, sleep apnea, or otherwise troubled sleep. Useful in dissipating and desiccating rage, anger, fear, and anxiety, and is a good stone for remembering dreams and past lives. Helps relieve tension both physical and emotional. Performs well when paired with rose quartz. Can bring change to a room or space, centering the room and its occupants when placed or hung in the center. Its color varies from a deep violet to pale lavender.

Ammonite:

Ammonite is excellent for amulets, and can dispel negative vibrations and negative energy. It lends clarity to the thinking and emotions of the bearer, and it helps to assist in weeding through extraneous details to identify what is truly important. Associated with the root chakra, it is good for centering, grounding, and meditation. It can assist in relaxation in stressful, chaotic situations, such as during anxiety attacks, or even during childbirth. It can also summon prosperity and abundance. The ammonite comes from the shell of an extinct mollusk the word ammonite is derived from Ammon, an Egyptian god who took the form of a ram.

Angelite:

This stone is excellent at balancing the emotions, and yoking the physical to the emotional. Is excellent to place in a yoga space or place of meditation. This crystal also acts as a magnet to familiars and totem animals, as well as astral travel and past lives regression. Very effective when used in work on the Throat Chakra, Angelite aids in expression, communication, and sharing. It emboldens others to communicate honestly with the bearer, and vice versa. It can aid in calming anxiety or hyper activity when worn on or near the throat chakra. Can be used to aid in focusing on universal vibrations, angels, ghosts, and otherworldly spirits. Angelite dispels anger, renews connections with Universal knowledge, and bestows confidence on the bearer to travel new and often lonely paths. In addition to assisting with the above metaphysical matters, it is helpful in hastening the curing of physical ailments. It is used for relieving throat inflammation and to balance the thyroid. It also repairs and acts as an anti-inflammatory on tissues and blood vessels. It is very useful for weight control, appetite control, and waste elimination. Can assist in resolving tensions between the physical body and subconscious mind.

Apache Tears:

These stones bring prosperity and good luck to the bearer. Apache tears also help the bearer to connect with the subconscious mind and resolve tensions between cognitions and emotions. It sheds light negative patterns and helps the bearer become aware them. It can assist in promoting behavioral change as new positive attitudes replace old, negative, repeated ones. The Apache tears are also said to balance the emotional nature and help the bearer balance trust with instincts of self-protectiveness. It can be carried as an amulet to foster success in business endeavors and money matters. It is best used at the Root Chakra for grounding and protection. When used in chakra work with the root chakra, it eases and releases pain, loss, sadness, and anger. Gently grounds and unblocks barriers to elimination of wastes and of negative vibrations. Helps heal ailments of the mind and spirit,

Apatite:

This stone is known for its abilities to help the bearer accelerate weight loss. Its helps to magnify the intensity of meditation. Blue and purple are used especially to heal and stimulate throat Chakra. Doing so will enhance abilities of self expression, communication, and patience. This will also accelerate the healing process for any ailments of the mouth, throat, or thyroid, as well as dulling the effects of high blood pressure and stuttering. Rumored too to strengthen muscle tissue and sharpen general motor skills, as well as promoting calcium absorption. Eases hypertension and restores clear thought. To reduce hunger, use the yellow ones in chakra work and meditation—the stone varies in color from white to brown to green to yellow. All are potent but the yellow one is best in matters of weight loss. Crystal form is hexagonal and glassy in appearance.

Apophylite:

These stones are clear, white, or light green striated crystals. They are helpful in assisting the bearer to connect with one's spirit self. Gazing into any of the colors can help strengthen, hasten, and deepen meditation, dream recall, and general relaxation. Also assists in sharpening skills of clairvoyance and astral travel. Green heals emotional scarring and brings ecstatic openness to even the most wounded of hearts if used on the heart Chakra. If used on the Third Eye it clears mental fuzziness and unblocks channels to connections with spirits and creatures of the other world. Mirrored Apophylite can bounce back intentions. Sending good vibrations and good energy into the mirrored variety of the stone can therefore have a protective effect. But keep your mirrored crystal in a safe place—if it falls into the hands of others, it can reflect the past motivations, energies, and meditative states of the user. Using it for gazing, however, can help the gazer get insight into his or her true, inner self and spiritual core. It provides a clear connection between the physical bodies and the astral bodies of its bearer. Mirror Apophylite is an extremely powerful crystal and will also sharpen the users' intuitive capacities by stimulating the Third Eye Chakra.

Aqua Aura:

This lovely gem is part man made, part natural. They are created by placing quartz pressurized chamber at high temperature and exposing the quartz to pure vaporized gold. The resulting blend creates the rich blue color called Aqua Aura. Despite the synthetic qualities of this stone, it is exceptionally powerful. It channels and collects vibrations to direct at to the bearer, serving to enhance intuition and communication. It can also serve to assist in reaching a relaxed state and sharpen perceptive abilities. Aqua aura is also said to act as a magnet for abundance— abundance of good energy, wealth, etc. It increases the ability to send energy and alter consciousness for meditation, telepathy, healing, and spellwork. It is best used on the throat chakra to boost immunity. If used on the Third Eye, it can soothe fevers and general anxiety and malaise. In addition to its abilities to magnify incoming energy, it can act as an amulet against bad energy or bad intentions. Psychic or psychological attacks from outside sources are quickly dissipated into pure pink energy, which can even serve to heal the person whose anger caused him or her to attack. The aqua aura quartz crystal will act as a conduit for expressive communication and positive energies, encouraging peace and guard against harmful vibrations.

Aquamarine:

This stone primarily channels water energy. It is particularly noteworthy for its ability to give courage to the bearer. No less potent, however, are its abilities to soothe, uplift, open the heart Chakra, and help the bearer connect with his or her core self in order to regenerate a sense of purpose. Best used in chakra work on the throat and heart. Those who travel on or over water should consider keeping one at all times for protection against psychic and physical harm. Those who travel over land could also benefit from having the stone as it helps the bearer stabilize the self when in unfamiliar surroundings and being bombarded by unfamiliar energies. Also, it can increase creativity and sharpen intuition. This is a particularly excellent stone for meditation as it quiets the mind and helps to reduce stress. Also can help open the heart to others in order to foster tolerance and understanding between strangers. When used on the throat chakra, it clears blocked communication and aids the user in verbal expression. In addition to assisting with psychic and mental well being, it has good results when used to strengthen the immune system, thymus, and lymph nodes. Also good for ADD/ADHD sufferers who need help fine tuning abilities to concentrate and block out distractions. Aquamarine is used to calm nerves. It can be used to clarify perception and strengthen the eyes, taste buds, lungs, teeth, throat, nose, mouth and ear canals. It allows for better breathing with allergies. This is good stone when convalescing from a prolonged malady, injury, or illness.

Aragonite:

This one can vary greatly in appearance, coming in shades purple, pink, brown and white, and hexagonal as well as needle shaped. Can assist the bearer into achieving a heightened state of meditation. It is also beneficial for uplifting spirits and general emotions. Simply using it to gaze into can help the gazer become more centered and true in realms of business, and can allow relationship challenges to be met with a clear head. This crystal can help the bearer balance ying and yang energies, and if used on the Third Eye chakra, can benefit the eyes, brain, nerves, and heart.

Aventurine:

An excellent prosperity talisman, aventurine channels abundance and brings good luck in money and matters of the heart. Can assist the bearer into getting in touch with his or her ability to give selfless love, seek truth, and share prosperity. If used as an amulet, aventurine protects the heart. If used on the Third Eye chakra, it enhances creativity and clears blocked channels to spirit guides. When used on the heart chakra, has a strong, potent ability to dissolve emotional blockages and wounds. Can help to balance the emotions, soothing anxiety and stress, and is one of the best stones to use for centering and meditation during times of acute stress and distraction. It can also be used in crystal layouts with effectiveness, blending well with the energies of other stones and crystals. It is a very versatile stone, able to heal physical and mental maladies. It can work to palliate ailments of the cardio-pulmonary system, and simulate the adrenal glands. It also can act as an aphrodisiac. If placed in bathwater, it can be a perfect way to smooth out anxiety and emotional blockages. If placed under a bed, it can stimulate sexual desire and openness. If used in conjunction with feng shui, it can help counteract incoming negative energy. Best placed in the North corner of a room to stimulate performance in matters of money, and in the West to help in matters of the heart. Aventurine may be green, orange, brown, yellow, or gray.

Azurite:

This beautiful stone comes in shades of blue and purple. When used on the brow and throat Chakra it can unblock channels of communication, and stimulate the bearer's ability to connect with the subconscious, remember dreams, and recall past lives. Can also serve to stimulate creativity, and decisiveness, while reducing susceptibility to being influenced by bad energies. When used on the throat chakra, it can stimulate the regenerative processes in the thyroid, sinus, skin, spleen, and nervous system. In addition to encouraging these improvements in the physical body, it can stimulate the robustness of the mental and etheric bodies. When used on the crown chakra, it can increase psychic abilities. Some say that this stone is perfect for pregnant women as it can stimulate the cells of developing babies in the womb. It also can help the bearer to let go of bitterness from the past, and open his or her heart to accept the future. Cultivates the ability to reach into the subconscious and engage in reflection of the self, cleansing the mind and making one more capable of insight and pure thought. Helps one recognize inner strength. Benefits the spleen, thyroid, bones, and skin. This stone can also be used in stone layouts as it blends well with other stones and gems, and is good for meditation.

B

Barite/Barium:

Barium is a white or colorless mineral which can have hints of blue, brown, gray, red or yellow. Barite is particularly useful for connecting with dream states and allowing the bearer to remember dreams and past lives. Also useful for the physical body, it can help cleanse the system of toxins, soothe an upset stomach, and help break behavior patterns associated with substance abuse. The Blue variety of Barite is best used to stimulate verbal communication as well as instill courage.

Beryl Family:

Beryl includes aquamarine, emeralds, golden or yellow beryl, heliodors and morganite. Members of this family assist their possessors in filtering out distractions, irrelevant information, bad energy, and extraneous sensory stimulation. As such, it can dissipate stress and anxiety. When used on the crown chakra, the blue beryl stones can stimulate communication. Green ones, when used on the throat chakra, stimulate spiritual healing. The pink ones, when used on the heart chakra, re-awaken romantic love. Gold and white varieties of this stone, when used on the solar plexus, support spiritual growth.

All varieties of the stone can help cure ailments of the stomach and intestines, including ulcers, nausea, acid reflux, and eating disorders. It also can help sufferers of exhaustion, depression, and listlessness. Gazing into these stones benefits the mind, nervous system, spine and bones. When used on the solar plexus, all varieties aid the elimination organs such as the kidneys, liver, and intestines. Helps strengthen the circulatory and pulmonary systems, making them more resistant to toxins and pollutants. Hang these stones in the center of any room to encourage peace, and in the southwest to strengthen relationships.

Bloodstone

This potent stone is associated with honesty and integrity. It can be used both to promote a calm, tranquil atmosphere, or to revitalize insufficient energy and invigorate the bearer. As such, this is a great stone for mental exhaustion and depression. A potentially excellent addition to a prosperity spread or spell, it attracts prosperity, abundance and good luck. Use on the heart chakra will benefit sufferers of anxiety; use on the root chakra will help those seeking prosperity. As can be guessed by the name, the bloodstone is also extremely useful for issues surrounding blood and circulation.

Bloodstone is an immune stimulator and can clean the blood of bad energy, and neutralize toxins. It is very popular amongst those who suffer from acute menstrual cramps, anemia, blood clots, hemorrhoids, cervical cancer, and hormonal imbalance. It is also beneficial to those suffering from Reynard's Syndrome. Placing the stone on the solar plexus when in meditation can help purify toxic blood and detoxify the kidneys, liver, and spleen. It can be placed in a bowl of water or in bath water to promote restful sleep, and can be placed anywhere to diffuse negative energy. The green color is caused by actinolite and the red patches are from iron oxide.

Boji Stones:

These unassuming stones are grey-brown discs. Despite their modest appearance, these stones have a very potent ability to ground, balance the body's electromagnetic field, and dissipate bad energies. Holding one stone in each hand while meditating can reduce or even get rid of chronic pain. For best results, stones must be charged after use by placing them in direct sunlight. The stones also must not be stored together, or paired with tiger's eye.

Brass:

This household metal has the ability to flatten and ground energy. It can dull and block all forms of energy and vibration. Though it may be used as shield, it is not an effective filter and will dull all incoming energies and vibrations, reducing sensitivity and awareness. It is, however, useful as a blood cleanser and a phlegmatic for those that find themselves over stimulated by psychic waves and energies.

C

Calcite:

This common crystal can vary greatly in appearance, coming in shades of white, gray, black, green, yellow, blue, brown, and red. All colors are beneficial for the kidneys, liver, bones, and joints, and for sharpening mental clarity. Placing calcite under the bed can help with dream recall. Also, wearing it while reading can help the reader retain more information. Athletes may find the stone especially useful because of its abilities to strengthen the bones and joints that are stressed or injured. This is a very important stone for any rituals involving healing or regeneration.

Lime Green Calcite:

This variation of the crystal promotes tranquility, soothes restlessness, and encourages introspection. A powerful psychic booster, it helps the bearer remember dream imagery, pursue astral travel and recall past lives. It also can clear toxins, fumes, and negativity from the physical body. This stone gets quickly saturated and will require rinsing if being used to draw out toxins.

Gold or Yellow Calcite:

This is an excellent stone to aid in meditation. When used on the heart chakra, it is invigorating to both mind and body. It is strongly recommended for those seeking to fine tune the art of astral projection. When used on the crown chakra, it can benefit the bones. If placed in a bath, it can also aid in the detoxification of the kidneys, pancreas, and spleen. It is also rumored to help arthritis.

Blue Calcite

This color calcite is particularly useful for easing back pain. Placing the stone in a warm bath or in a hot water bottle can help muscle cramps as well.

Carnelian:

If used correctly, carnelian can encourage boldness, initiative, dramatic abilities, assertiveness and affability. Its secondary capabilities include an ability to stimulate appetite, encourage gregariousness, and intensify emotions. It is the stone of passion and sexuality and is best used with the sacral chakra. If merely carried or worn as a talisman, the stone helps the bearer feel anchored and comfortable with even the most chaotic of surroundings.

Carnelian can also improve motivation and drive, helping the bearer forge a more efficient path to success in career or personal matters. Carnelian is one of the most helpful crystals for healing depression, stress, and emotional maladies that have accumulated in the aura and manifest themselves by affecting the health of the physical body. Carnelian can cleanse and purify the blood, liver, and kidneys, while simultaneously stimulating appetite, passion, sexuality, physical energy, fertility, and overall boisterousness. As such, this is not the best stone for hyperactive people or sufferers of ADD. Carnelian is said to strongly influence the reproductive organs of both sexes, and can be excellent to quell cramps or lower back problems. Carnelian is a form of quartz. Carnelian comes in a variety of colors ranging from red to orange to dark brown.

Celestite:

These white, clear, or light blue cluster crystals have a gentle energy that soothes frazzled nerves, quiets the mind, and allows the bearer to get centered in even the noisiest, most distracting of environments. If used on the third eye, these crystals can help sufferers of anxiety. They can also help with meditation, and promote serenity, harmony, stillness, and a clear channel to the spirit and other world.

When used on the throat chakra, encourages openness, tranquility, and calmness, as well as helping sharpen the sense of smell, and hearing.

Cerussite:

This stone ranges in color from clear to opaque white to brown. It can assist the bearer gain confidence and to feel capable. While encouraging confidence and self-love, it also inspires humility and good listening skills. Use in meditation can help the bearer separate what cannot change from what can be changed. The stone can also help sufferers of heart break and emotional scarring to heal and let go of anger and bitterness. When placed under the bed, it can relieve some of the symptoms of insomnia and restlessness. When used on the crown chakra, it can cleanse the central nervous system, promoting coordination, and increase in fine motor skills.

Chalcedony:

This crystal is a type of quartz that most often comes in gray but also is found shades of white, black, blue, and brown. Using the stone in meditation or gazing can help ease self-doubts, and promote introspection. Placing the stone in the bath can alleviate the trauma of bad dreams, as well as help clear up problems related to the eye, gall bladder, bones, spleen, blood, and veins. Passing chalcedony over an open wound will speed its healing, and can promote mending of all kinds. Unlike most crystals, it's not especially important that it's cleaned after use because it has such strong cleansing qualities of its own. As a secondary use, this crystal aids in the development of maternal feelings, and can help breastfeeding mothers produce more milk.

Charoite:

This stone is known as the transformer. It helps us take a fresh approach to old information and old patterns. It is believed to open the heart, allow inspiration to strike, and open the third eye. The stone can facilitate a better connection with the spirit world. It also is believed that this stone accelerates emotional healing. Some find it a great stone for entity release. This is a fairly versatile stone, but to stimulate psychic powers and the openness of the third eye, use the stone on the heart, third eye, and crown charkas. Use in this fashion can help the recipient of its energy with gaining insight and releasing fear of the new. This also can be used as an amulet against negative energies and vibrations. It can also assist in the development of foresight and intuitive vision. This crystal also has several benefits to the physical body. It is recommended for alcohol and food detoxification. This stone is said to regulate blood pressure, as well as regenerate fatigues cells. It also can be used to treat insomnia and restless leg syndrome. Putting charoite under the bed or pillow can help bring relief to almost all sleep disorders, particularly if used with amethyst. Charoite can be bright lavender or dark purple with occasional streaks of white, gray or black.

Chiastolite:

This powerful crystal evens out the balance between the bearer's optimism and practicality. It can magnify of spiritual and psychic awareness, and diffuse negativity. It can be used to clear connections to the spirit world, and is perfect for gazing in order to accelerate achievement of a heightened state of meditation. It also can help the bearer adjust to particularly acute times of change. This stone has a reputation for astral journeys and is used as a gateway into the metaphysical and the paranormal, allowing the bearer to overcome fear of the "other" and the unknown, and progress into a state of total awareness. Chiastolite can also help us get in touch with our true purpose. When used on the root chakra, it is grounding and fine tunes basic, primal instincts, and helps us get in touch with our rawest selves. During illness, it helps to maintain focus on matters of the spirit, lessens fever, regulates blood flow and repairs cellular damage. It also can help settle chemical imbalances in the brain.

Chinese Writing Stone:

This is a limestone matrix with andalusian crystal steaks. It is a mineral that can be a powerful enabler of accessing lives, and receive messages from ancestors and kindred spirits. It is and excellent stone for helping the bearer achieve a dream state. It is a stone inspiring affirmation, alignment, and spiritual commitment. It helps one to adjust to change, and sort out fine line between the desire to improve oneself and the desire to accept oneself.

Chrysocolla/Gem Silica:

This bluish green stone has a gentle, soothing energy. When used on the heart chakra it can help flush out and heal emotional blockage, giving sufferers of heartbreak and anguish the ability to make peace with the past, and regard the future with flexibility and patience. The stone can be used daily to bring light, love, and healing into a space. If used with the throat chakra, it can help the reticent in expressing feelings. It also can inspire creativity and tone the thyroid. In meditation, it helps slow heart rate, even out spikes in blood sugar, and encourages emotional balance. When used in a hot bath it can absorb pain and heat from inflammation or infection. When used for meditative purposes, or in reiki, it is excellent in its ability to cleanse the auric field. It is best used for healing the physical body when used in an effort to combat arthritis and other bone diseases. It also can soothe organs of the digestive tract, and act as a palliative to ulcers. This stone may be especially useful to public speakers and vocalists because of its ability to promote expression through the voice.

Chrysoprase:

This translucent green stone can inspire greater flexibility, wisdom, generosity, and self-confidence when used on the heart chakra. When used on the crown chakra, it can help alleviate depression, self-absorption, and excessive preoccupation with sex. If used on the third eye, it can bring personal insight and stimulate an awareness of the emotional vibrations of others. When used in meditative work, it can inspire creativity. Either sex can benefit from its ability to encourage fertility and abundance. When placed in a hot bath, it can help gout, schizophrenia, and vision problems.

Citrine:

This stone is very versatile for matters of the mind and spirit. It can be used to inspire emotional clarity, fine-tune problem solving, stimulate the memory, reinforce will power, encourage optimism, and reinforce self-discipline. If used on the crown chakra, it will help to reduce anxiety, fear and depression. Citrine is unique because unlike most crystals, it's not necessary for it to be cleaned or rinsed of negative energy after use. A citrine stone absorbs, dissipates, grounds, and dissolves negative energy, and as such, is a perfect amulet. Citrine crystal energy can be described as invigorating and positive. One only has to hold the crystal to physically be touched by its brilliance and potency, which energizes and charges its surroundings. When used in meditation, the stone can guide you into harnessing and making the most use of your unique talents. The bearer of these stones is quickly able to enter a state of peaceful, calm, self love, and becomes not only immune to negativity, but open to constructive criticism. The stone can also invigorate and stimulate the sexual and reproductive organs of both sexes when used in chakra work on the Sacral Chakra, the Solar plexus Chakra and Crown Chakra. When used on then crown chakra, the stone can help alleviate anxiety and fear of the unknown. The orange colored citrines are most beneficial to stimulate creativity and arousal, whereas the yellowish varieties of citrine are more beneficial to the digestive system. Citrine energizes, cleanses, and balances the aura. All varieties, in addition to stimulating the sex organs, ease difficulties with digestion, and reduce the ill effects of some food allergies The stone can also detoxify the kidneys, liver, urinary system, intestines. Citrine promotes physical activity, which in turn improves digestion and helps the cleansing organs. It can also be used on the abdomen for aiding waste elimination, and alleviating menstrual cramps.

Cobalt-Calcite:

This stone has a gentle energy that can fill its surroundings with love, patience, and compassion. It is incredibly soothing, and the bearer can use the stone in order to experience a respite from particularly strong or unpleasant emotions. In general, it promotes mental and emotional balance. Using the stone on the heart chakra can allow for emotional and spiritual healing. Also is good for cleansing the aura.

Copper:

This metal is a very good energy conductor. It can magnify the intensity of psychic vibrations, promotes healing, and magnifies gem electrical energy. If worn or carried on bare skin, it detoxes the joints and soothes arthritis, rheumatism, and other inflammation problems. If used on the third chakra, it can tone the stomach and intestines. Use on the heart can inspire the heart to warm, as well as release resentment and pent up anger. If used on the solar plexus, it can aid in exhaustion recovery, and circulation. Overall, it can intensify both sun and lunar energy. For best results, copper should be charged in the moon and sunlight. Carrying it can help stabilize the metabolism and improve the immune system. The blood also benefits from copper, and is purified, and arteries are rejuvenated. When worn near the throat, as a pendant or as part of an amulet, it can be beneficial for the lungs, improving the exchange of oxygen and filtering out pollutants. Copper can benefit the tissue and mucous membranes, tremendously, causing them to absorb more moisture and become less susceptible to irritation.

Coral:

Coral encourages diplomacy and teamwork, soothes turbulent emotions, and brings tranquility to the spirit self. It also facilitates intuition, imagination, visualization, expediting and accelerating the absorption of knowledge. When used on the crown chakra, it can strengthen both the circulatory system and the bones. When used on the third eye chakra, it stimulates tissue regeneration and nourishes white blood cells. If used in meditation, it can help with disorders of the spine, nervous system and thalamus. Different colors of coral can be used alone, in combination, or all together, and all have roughly the same attributes, with some minor variations. All coral is particularly useful to treat ailments of the bones and blood, such as arthritis and anemia. It also can help soothe sufferers of a variety of mental illnesses.

Red and Orange Coral:

These warmer colors stimulate the root chakra for sexual energy and fertility. It can also energize emotions surrounding sex and childbearing. On a physical level, these colors are particularly beneficial to the blood, heart, reproductive system, thyroid, metabolism, and nervous system. These are not the best colors, however, for sufferers of anxiety or nervousness.

Pink Coral:

Pink coral is particularly beneficial to the heart, opening the emotions and encouraging openness.

White Coral

White coral has the most gentle, soothing energy. It serves to alleviate stress, anxiety, and jittery nerves. This color is particularly useful for sufferers of PTSD.

Blue Coral

This color is particularly useful to singers and public speakers as it activates and energizes the Throat Chakra, improves communication abilities, soothes throat ailments, and cleans the mucous membranes. When used on the third eye, it can enhance psychic awareness.

Corundum:

This mineral can assist the bearer into gaining insight to the unknown and spirit world. It increases intuitive awareness, stimulates ambition, and boosts confidence. It is good for PMS and other mood disorders as it calms irascibility and irritation, and dispels anger. It also smoothes the skin, hastens the healing of eye disorders, and brings peace to the aura.

Creedite:

This stone stimulates the body's own ability to self-purify and detoxify. It is particularly useful for blood detoxification. It is also good at opening channels of intuitive communication. Will also benefit the nervous system by aiding in the transmission of messages from the brain to the nerves, improving motor skills and coordination.

Cuprite:

This beautiful red stone opens the energy flow of the root and spleen chakras, strengthening Kundalini energy. It can also be used on the heart chakra to strengthen resolve and will power. The bearer will experience significant benefits to the thymus, heart, blood, and the metabolism will also be balanced. Many also experience significant upticks in stamina and overall energy levels. This stone works primarily to get us in touch with our yang energy, allowing both sexes to benefit from increased awareness of masculine energies in their selves and lives. Using cuprite during meditation can assist in the ability to recall past lives. If used on the hearth chakra, it helps the heart and blood, muscles, tendons, and skeletal system. Because of its focus on yang energy, those with issues with fathers or male authority figures could benefit from incorporating cuprite into gem layouts.

D

Danburite:

This clear crystal radiates pure, white energy, filling the physical body, mind, and aura with good energy and vibrations. This is an excellent addition to any purification rituals, or ritual baths. Use on the crown chakra will fill the heart with joy. Use in meditation mind, nervous system, life force, awareness. It is excellent for sufferers of depression, anxiety, or PTSD, and is perfect to carry as a talisman during particularly stressful or difficult times.

Desert Rose:

This light brown gypsum stone grounds the bearer, bringing him/her increased awareness, perception, and mental vision. It is perfect to use in meditation as it quiets the mind, and can assist in the recalling of dreams and past lives. Additionally, it encourages emotional flexibility, strengthens decisions, aligns the spine, and removes energy blockages. Some also claim that it is beneficial for sufferers of epilepsy.

Diamond:

It is all too easy to get distracted by this stone's monetary value and forget that it is a powerful conductor of energy. This is an especially good gem to use in conjunction with other crystals and gems in order to strengthen their various energies. If used with an Aquamarine, a diamond will increase the aquamarine's cleansing properties. When worn or carried alone, it increases the energy of the bearer, both positive and negative. Diamonds also benefit sufferers of glaucoma, and are said to benefit the testicles. In all cases, the stone needs to touch the skin in order to be effective. Simply wearing a diamond ring perched on its setting will not be of much benefit. Emeralds, amethysts, and quartz stones are particularly strengthened when used in combination with diamonds. Diamonds alone amplify the attitudes of the bearer. They also soak and preserve energy very easy, so they must be cleaned and recharged thoroughly after each used, or if touched by others.

Diopside/Enstatite:

These gems, though different, have the same properties, and are hence are mentioned in the same spot. They invigorate the heart chakra with a heightened sense of love, commitment to the self, and humility. They also tone the heart, lungs, and arteries. Using these stones in meditation will yield an increased awareness of the heart chakra. Both also benefit the circulatory system and aid in elimination. Mental clarity and steadfastness result from healing layouts that include these stones.

Dioptase:

These crystals, though small, have powerful energy. If worn on the skin, the bearer will feel their energy deep in the Heart Chakra . Using these stones in meditation will hasten the release of heartache stemming from abuse, neglect, or love gone bad. If used on the heart chakra, they can infuse the heart with strength, courage, and openness, allowing even the most wounded to open up and love again. These stones free the bearer from the constraints of self-consciousness and insecurity, encouraging sincerity, emotional balance, and spiritual health. If used on the solar plexus, the lungs, heart, blood, and circulatory systems can benefit tremendously.

Dolomite:

This is an excellent stone for those suffering from heartbreak or depression, as it mutes loneliness and dulls anxiety. In addition, it encourages the bearer to be open to giving and receiving, and can give the bearer a boost in energy and creative juices. This stone also encourages charitable actions. Additionally, it can block or prevent "energy leakages". It can be used for energy alignment, and balance. The stone is good for the physical body as well as the spiritual, strengthening the bones, teeth, muscles, and joints. Placing the stone in the center of a room or space can balance and ground the room's energy.

E

Eilat Stone:

This powerful, semi-precious gem has an ability to store and conduct energy, both bad and good. In addition, the stone has an exceptional ability to absorb pain, and as such, is a great talisman for sufferers of chronic arthritis and other types of diseases from which there is little relief. It excels in healing the heart chakra, and benefits the circulatory system. When placed on the solar plexus during meditation, it aligns the chakras, and harmonizes the spiritual and physical bodies. When used in meditation, it can bring peace of heart and ease of self expression. It is also very good at balancing aspects of ying and yang energy in a room or an individual. This crystal is also strongly recommended for whole body healing. It flushes out and heals both physical and mental stress and pain. It benefits the physical body in soothing inflammation in the sinuses, and mouth, and hastens bone and tissue regeneration. It can out pain and cool a fever.

Eilat is used primarily anywhere to help bring balance. Place it in the center of a room or space to encourage good health, balance of ying and yang, and spirituality.

Elestial:

This member of the quartz family encourages psychic abilities, openness to higher self, and openness to higher power. This stone can also stimulate the crown chakra. In some individuals, the stone can be extremely helpful for matter of intuition and spirituality, but for others, it can intensify lower thoughts, such as preoccupation with the self and material riches. After the bearer gets used to the stone's energy, however, the bearer can overcome these hurdles and use the stone to tremendous benefit. The stone also is good for healing brain cell damage stemming from alcohol and drug abuse, or head trauma. This can also be used to enhance energy flow between chakras.

Emerald:

This gem is a symbol of love and good fortune. It can promote prosperity, abundance, growth, peace, harmony, patience, love, fidelity and honesty. It used against negative energy and when used for gazing, can be helpful for divination. When used on the heart chakra, it can help the user get in touch with the innermost self and innermost desires. Emerald provides inspiration and helps those in need of balance, healing, and patience. It can also ease the effects of depression, and helps with insomnia and other sleep afflictions. When worn directly on the skin, the bearer can achieve physical, emotional, and mental equilibrium. Though very effective when used alone, emeralds also respond well to being used in conjunction with diamonds. Emerald energy dissipates quickly, so it is best when used in short periods of time. It must be cleansed and then recharged after each use. This crystal is the most recommended stone for respiratory issues, heart difficulties, swollen lymph nodes, labor/delivery, eyesight, and the aura. It is an excellent general healer. It can also act as an excellent blood detoxifier, evening out spikes in blood sugar for diabetics and hypoglycemics. When used in meditation or for gazing, emeralds improve psychic abilities, raises consciousness, and help the individual attain spiritual balance and alignment.

Epidote:

This deep green strengthens the circulatory system and promotes over-all health, cardiopulmonary well-being, and good energy. It also promotes courage and stamina.

F

Flint:

This gray, white, black, red, or brown stone is found in all countries around the world. It was beneficial to the entire body. All tissue, internal or external, will be helped, but especially the cardiopulmonary and cleansing systems. It can give a strong boost of optimism to one's world view and is extremely helpful for persons who have been diagnosed with degenerative, chronic, or incurable diseases.

Fluorite:

This stone comes in a variety of colors: white, brown, blue, yellow, purple, red, or clear. It is a good all-around balancer and healer, opening the heart and third eye chakras to give the bearer clarity and insight into matters of the heart and spirit. It is also beneficial to the physical body, toning the spleen, and strengthening the bones and teeth. It also is an excellent detoxifier of the blood and helps to alleviate sleep ailments such as insomnia or restless leg syndrome. People with arthritis, rheumatism, or spinal injuries have can experience some relief from their symptoms when they include Fluorite in their healing and health regimens. It can also act as an aphrodisiac and help the bearer reinvigorate his or her sexual drive. When used in meditation, it can help the bearer become more acutely aware of the higher levels of reality, and can have a grounding effect to prevent over stimulation of the psyche.

Fuchsite:

This stone promotes lightheartedness, friendliness, compassion, and recovery from spiritually damaging experiences.

G

Garnet:

This gem stimulates creativity, and passion, and can also offer tremendous benefits to the circulatory system. It comes in a variety of different shades and colors. Red can benefit the root chakra. It warms, energizes the emotional and physical body, and grounds the wearer. It can also help sufferers of exhaustion and low blood pressure, detoxing and strengthening the blood and kidneys. Red also stimulates passion, life force and sexuality, and can increase fertility. It has a lot of Yang energy so avoid this color if you suffer from excess anger, impatience, high blood pressure, or restlessness. Orange: can stimulate the pituitary gland, promoting the awareness of past lives. It benefits the third eye chakra. Green Garnets are healing stones. Garnets teach patience and constancy and are not to be used lightly. They sharpen self-perception and help calm anger, resentment, and anxiety.

Geodes:

Geodes are spherical stones. They contain cavities lined with crystalline structures that grow towards the center. They usually contain quartz, amethyst, citrine, or calcite. These powerful stones facilitate astral travel. When used in meditation, they can allow the bearer to have clarity and honesty in decision making. Geodes provide a powerful connection to the higher plane, stimulate communication skills, and facilitate psychic awareness. They can be used with much benefit to treat disorders of the hands, feet, lungs and nerves.

Gold:

This is an excellent all-purpose, gem amplifier and electrical conductor, and can give tremendous benefits when used on the solar plexus and Heart Chakra. It can align the chakras and the physical and spiritual body, and tones the digestive system. It attracts abundance, fertility, and prosperity, and it can stores and amplify the energy of the wearer, and of other stones. White gold combines the sun and moon's energy, and as such, acts as a higher conductor and amplifier of both. White gold is a regenerator, helping one renew oneself. It benefits the nervous system and helps sufferers of nervous disorders such as anxiety. It can aid in digestion and helps the body in the proper assimilation of food, while also assisting the body's natural methods of elimination in working effectively. It can also help control chemical imbalances. It works well with all crystals and gemstones and can be used in conjunction with copper and silver. Gold colored gold (as opposed to white gold) is ruled by the sun and therefore imparts yang energy to the wearer, and to the crystals and minerals that are mounted in it.

Goldstone:

Goldstone is a man-made stone and as such, is pretty much a type of glass with glittery material in it.

Granite:

Granite is a sacred and powerful stone. It can be an excellent amulet as it has strong protective qualities. It is made mostly of quartz and feldspar and has properties that are a blend of those stones. This stone can help those whose psychic energy is blocked. It encourages for diplomacy, discretion, and cooperativeness, and mutes negative vibrations and energies. Granite also has been used to strengthen the hair and alleviate ailments of the cranium and neck. If used in conjunction with Flint, it can act to stimulate cell and tissue regeneration. When used in meditative work, it can have a powerfully grounding effect.

H

Hawk's Eye:

This member of the quartz family can help the bearer gain perspective, and mutes emotions that are irrelevant or distracting to sound decision making. This is particularly true when used on the third eye chakra during meditation. The blue variety of the stone is particularly good for giving the bearer sharpened psychic abilities, and aiding in astral travel.

Hematite:

This is a great stone for grounding and is generally used on the root chakra to encourage centering. Hematite unifies scattered feelings, encourages mental clarity, and helps with concentration. It is therefore particularly useful for students or others that have to focus for long periods of time and remember lots of information. It also can work as a sleep aid. When used in meditation, it encourages will power and boldness. It has highly protective energy and helps boost low self-esteem. It restores equilibrium and stability, and brings our awareness to the physical body to help maintain a unified sense of self. Hematite can also be used at the base of the spine to support the kidneys and spleen. IT helps in tissue regeneration, and can alleviate the symptoms of anemia. Hematite can benefit those who need to emotionally recharge and regroup after experiencing trauma, childbirth, or an intense period of change. If placed in the center of a room, it can aid in balancing and grounding.

Herkimer Diamonds:

These crystals resemble Diamonds but are really Quartz. They are excellent to aid in visualization during meditation. If placed under the pillow, they can help with dream and past life recall. They are also excellent for astral travel. When used on the third eye chakra, this stone can bring on a particularly deep state of stillness and reflection. It amplifies positive energy and can be used as a bridge to stimulate energy flow between chakras, creating a strong, clear channel for psychic readings, divination, communication with spirit beings, and meditation. These stones also have powerful earth energy. They contain a large store of ecological memory that can be accessed those who can correctly tune in with the stone's strong vibrations. This crystal can raise the energy levels of those handling the stone, as well amplify the qualities of other stones. This stone works very well when used with amethyst, rose quartz, and hematite. It can be placed anywhere in a room or space in order to clear and move energy where there is vibrational stagnation. The stone must be cleaned and recharged often.

Hiddenite:

This is an excellent talisman for prosperity. It clears the heart chakra, allowing the bearer to let go of painful or difficult emotions. It has a particularly calming, soothing energy.

Howlite:

This stone can absorb stress, tension, anxiety, and other intense emotions. It works closely with the heart chakra, giving the bearer a renewed sense of patience and love for others. It also strengthens the bones, teeth, skin, and hair.

I

Iolite:

This blue-purple stone opens a pathway from the heart chakra to the crown chakra. It gives the wearer heightened visualization abilities, and if used during meditation, brings on peace and stillness. It is also good for helping the recently sober detox from drugs or alcohol, and solidifies a commitment to sobriety. Iolite is one of the best stones to use in psychic, healing, and spiritual activities, be it for meditation, gazing, or chakra work. It is also an excellent stone for meditation and astral travel.

Ivory:

Ivory comes from the bones and tusks of certain animals, many of which are on the brink of extinction and hunted down for their ivory. As such, it has such serious ecological ramifications that it is difficult to see the need to use ivory for spiritual work, particularly when other stones will suffice.

J

Jade:

Jade is a powerful talisman for health, wealth, and longevity stone. It can also be used in meditation to gain courage, wisdom, justice, mercy, emotional balance, stamina, love, fidelity, humility, generosity, peace, and harmony. It has a steady pulse of healing energy that is a blend of both ying and yang energies. Though usually thought of as a green stone, it is found in different colors and can be used on the appropriate Chakra based on its color. When used on the heart chakra, any color can be very beneficial to the heart in both physical and spiritual senses. It is a very protective stone and will keep its wearer out of harm's way. Jade has powerful earth energy and is a very humbling stone, helping the wearer ground him or herself. Jade benefits the physical body as well as the spiritual one, benefiting the cardiopulmonary system, the thymus, the immune system, the kidney, blood detoxification and nervous system. While all Jade has some healing influence, each color relates more specifically to certain ailments or organs. All colors, however, strengthen the body's filtration and cleansing systems and assists in the removal of toxins. If placed in the center area of a room, the room will become more harmonious and balanced.

Blue Jade:

Blue jade is a peaceful, subtle, and passive source of energy. This stone is perfect for those who meditate to relax and gain an inner serenity. It is great in gem layouts to soothe the energy of harsher, more intense stones.

Brown Jade:

Brown jade has a lot of earth energy. It is perfect to use for gazing, and for those who are in the throes of adjusting to a new environment.

Green Jade:

This is the most common form of jade, and it is particularly useful for calming the nervous system. The color green is representative of life, fertility, and growth. Use on the throat chakra can help the bearer channel passions in a constructive way, and ease self-expression.

Lavender Jade:

This color of jade is particularly useful for those seeking to get in touch with innermost emotions. If used on the third eye chakra, it can help the bearer learn restraint and subtlety in matters of emotional expression and perception.

Red Jade:

This is a passionate and vibrationally active stone. It is not recommended for those suffering from anxiety or other nervous disorders as it can have such a stimulating influence as to agitate or stress out the wearer. Those, however, who face challenges in constructively getting in touch with and expressing anger can benefit from using red jade. It also is a powerful stone for releasing tension.

White or Cream Jade:

This stone helps filter out emotional distraction so that the bearer can focus. It is also beneficial to those suffering from chronic eye diseases or infections.

Yellow and Orange Jade:

These vibrant stones give off strong vibrations that will infuse the wearer with joy and happiness. They also benefit the skin, and help the circulatory system.

Jasper:

This is a grounding stone that filters out distracting emotions. It is very useful for the overly anxious or emotional. It is used for grounding and protection. It is particularly effective when used on the root chakra. It can help with tissue regeneration, and vitamin and mineral assimilation. Darker colors are the best for those looking for a grounding stone. It is a good addition to potions and elixirs because it will not over-stimulate any energy center. Jasper works well in conjunction with opals, and can act as an amulet. When placed in the center of a room, it will have a noticeable grounding effect.

Brown Jasper:

Though all forms of jasper have a grounding element, this form is the strongest grounder. It is infused with earth energy. It benefits respiratory ailments that result from air pollution. It the immune system and assist in filtering pollutants and toxins from the lungs and blood. It is also good for people who wish to use meditation to help relive past events through regression or analysis.

Green Jasper:

This color is great when used for work on the respiratory system to repair damage from smoking or pollution. It's also good for those working on hypersensitivity. Has a salubrious effect on ailments of the upper torso, digestive tract, and the cleansing organs.

Red Jasper:

This stone is good for detoxifying the blood and strengthening the circulatory system. As such, it has a beneficial effect on the liver as well because it's so rich in blood. It can be used as an amulet protection, or as a talisman to bring courage and energy. It can help people who suffer from anemia, as well as people who bruise easily when used on the root chakra, this stone can bring health, prosperity, and security to the bearer. The color for the root chakra is red and it is grounded with your power. Red stones are usually projecting stones and are used to destroy disease, strengthen the conscious self, and bring courage, strength, physical energy, luck, and success.

Yellow Jasper:

Yellow jasper is beneficial to the endocrine glands and the urinary tract. It is a good addition to elixirs as it brings on a feeling of robustness and good health. It also tones the stomach, intestines, liver, and spleen. It is a grounding stone. Also used for communication, inspiration, protection, visualization, travel, digestion, nervous system, skin problems, breathing disorders. Yellow Jasper can be used at the Solar Plexus Chakra to stimulate yang energy, and awareness of the self. It will also stimulate the metabolism, and benefit motor skills and general agility. Yellow stones are considered projecting stones and are used to destroy disease, strengthen the conscious mind, inspire courage, increase strength, give physical energy, and attract success.

Jet:

This is fossilized organic matter that appears to be a rock or stone. It's actually a form of petrified wood, and as such, has a lot of earth energy and can absorb large quantities of energy, both negative and positive. If used correctly, it can help draw out negative energy. It is great for people who suffer from anxiety, agoraphobia, or nervousness. It can also control spikes in mood and alleviate the symptoms of both mania and depression. It good for all-purpose stimulation of the psyche, and can guide those in a quest for spiritual enlightenment. It is complemented by silver, so a silver setting is ideal for a necklace or pendant.

K

Kundalini Quartz:

This member of the quartz family contains some hematite. Kundalini, as yogis know, is the energy stored in the spine, most potent at the base of the spine. It can also be described as the experience of the individual when absorbing and interacting with universal energy and inspiration. Also known as black phantom quartz, they are sometimes called Kundalini Quartz because of their ability to raise one's energy level from the base chakra (1st) through the crown chakra (7th) and above. This is a very powerful, energizing, invigorating stone. The hematite grounds, the smoky quartz moves primal energies in the body, and the quartz transmits and amplifies energy. Raising the Kundalini will lead one to a more spiritual, less ego-centered life. It can be achieved through meditation, yoga, or both.

Kunzite:

Kunzite is a powerful, high level stone. It can be used as an amulet to ward off negative energy, while at the same time acting as a talisman that attracts positive thoughts. If used in chakra work, it can benefit the emotions and the spirit by being used on the heart chakra. It assists the bearer in experiencing unconditional, boundless love and compassion. It is wonderful for those learning how to trust the world again after going through a traumatic experience. It can help balance tendencies to give with tendencies to take. If used on the third eye or crown chakra, it can encourage the onset of a deep, meditative state that can yield dream recall, past lives recall, or divination. It is excellent for emotional healing, and for those who wish to be more centered. It reduces depression, even off spikes in mood, soothe stress, and counter the hazardous effects of excessive exposure to UV rays. It is also good for the veins, arteries, and lungs. It is excellent in gem layouts that seek to mellow out the energy in a space or room

Kyanite:

Kyanite has powerful earth energy and is a good grounding stone that encourages centeredness and tranquility. Blue kyanite works well with the throat and heart chakras to encourage expression, emotional awareness, and communication. If used on the third eye, it can raise the bearer's ability to tune into changes in energy, as well as cultivate meditation, divination, and dream recall skills. It can bring on vivid dreams and helps us get in touch with our subconscious. While all varieties are grounding, black is the most grounding, and is best used in chakra work at the root chakra, it is a conduit for "rogue energy", focusing the energy of the bearer into a desirable direction. As such, it is great for sufferers of ADD/ADHD, hyperactivity, or mania. If used in the center of a room, it will ground and focus the energy of the room or space.

L

Labradorite (Spectrolite) :

This stone comes in a variety of colors, including green, blue, and yellow. It can take on an iridescent quality. This is a great stone for sufferers of insomnia, anxiety, or other sleep disorders. It also boosts self esteem by bringing the bearer's awareness to the self and its gifts. It can open energy flow through the chakras, and if used in gazing, can help bring on a state of heightened self awareness. This fragile stone should only be cleaned in spring water. It is a good accompaniment to other forms of therapy as it encourages self-assessment and self-awareness.

Lapis Lazuli:

This vibrant blue stone is excellent for use in meditation and chakra work. It can bring on awareness of a higher power, intuition, and connection to higher self if used on the third eye chakra. It also can clear blocked channels of energy and augment the bearer's receptiveness to vibrations and emotions. If used for gazing, it can quiet the restless mind without causing drowsiness or witlessness. It encourages all forms of self-expression and balances awareness of the other with awareness of the self. It has a salubrious effect on anxiety, restlessness, insomnia, hyperactivity, reticence, PTSD, agoraphobia, and social anxiety disorder. It can help those with hearing loss, stuttering problems, and headaches. It is beneficial to the physical body, cleaning the respiratory system, toning the digestive system, and soothing the nervous system. It is a good stone for ridding the blood and respiratory system of toxins, and for boosting the immune system. It can help align the chakras so that energy can flow properly. It can increase psychic abilities and will open the third eye. It should be worn as close to the throat as possible to draw energy up through the chakras.

Larimar:

This gentle stone usually comes in a shade of light blue. It has lots of water energy, and brings the tranquility of the sea to a room or space. It dulls the negative effects of hurt, fear, depression, pain of loss, and everyday stress. It encourages open-mindedness, simplicity, and ying energy. It is beneficial to the physical body in that it helps cool a fever, draws out inflammation and infection, and helps sunburns heal quicker. When used on the heart or third eye chakras, it can help battle anxiety, stress, fear, and self-doubt.

Lepidolite:

Lepidolite is actually a combination of lithium and mica. It varies in texture and color, and can be silvery or opaque, in shades of purple or lavender. The stone has a very gentle, soothing energy that calms the bearer and infuses the room with ying energy. It eases intensity of negative emotions, stress, mood swings, depression, manic-depression, anxiety, addiction withdrawal, and general nervousness. When used on the third eye chakra, it can bring about a renewed sense of hope, self-forgiveness, and self love. It is great for treating sleep disorders, and for encouraging emotional balance. It can also help alleviate disorders of the skin, such as acne and eczema. This fragile stone should only be cleaned and recharged using sunlight, moonlight, or spring water. Salt water, even sea water, may cause the stone to crumble.

Lodestone:

This stone is a metallic-looking black color, and is a natural magnet. It behaves much like hematite in that it encourages grounding, clear thinking, and focus. With its natural magnetic energy, it draws toxins from the blood, unblocks energy bottlenecks, relieves pain from energy meridians, and tones the pancreas, and lower glands.

Sometimes these stones are referred to as "lodestones" or "healing stones"

M

Malachite:

This stone has a very intense, steady, pulsing energy due in part to its high copper content. If used on the third eye chakra, it can stimulate physical and psychic vision, as well as focus and concentration. If used on the heart or solar plexus, if can benefit the stomach, liver, lungs, immune system, and circulation, and have a salubrious effects on damages caused by air pollution. If used in meditation or in a hot bath, it can releases and draws out pain, inflammation, depression, and anger, and heals emotional blockages. It can also be a good tool to use for cleaning the auric field as it quickly soaks up undesirable negative energy. It also absorbs ambient radiation, such as that emanating from a TV, radio, computer, or microwave. It can benefit a household tremendously to have one in each corner of any room that contains electrical appliances, as it will absorb the extra electromagnetism and radiation. Because these stones are so absorbent, they must be cleaned daily. When worn as jewelry or an amulet, it can magnify both the positive and negative energy of the wearer, so it is a great accessory for times of tremendous self-confidence. It is useful for relaxation, and soothes the manifestations of nervous disorders as well as stimulating brain cell regeneration. It is said to be particularly useful for those suffering from schizophrenia. Its benefits to the physical body include the strengthening of the optic nerve, toning of the pancreas, and regeneration of damaged cells in the spleen and thyroid. People living near nuclear power plants should keep pieces of Malachite in their homes. Raw malachite should be kept out of the reach of children because it can be highly toxic.

Malachite/Azurite:

This hybrid stone naturally blends two very beneficial stones. Malachite and azurite are the same chemical, practically, Copper Carbonate. Malachite has the ability to draw out positive or negative energy, and Azurite is soothing and calming to the spirit. Together they have the ability to neutralize rogue energy and produce a sense of tranquility and stillness. Sleep will improve and you will be better able to interpret your dreams.□

Marascite:

This silvery-gray metallic stone is actually iron sulfide. It is infused with earth energy and is one of the most grounding of all stones. It is particularly useful on the root chakra in order to align the chakra, encourage energy to flow properly, and to ground and focus excess energy. It encourages scattered, hyperactive people to center their energy and make the most productive use of it. It also is beneficial to improving concentration and memory. As such, those who do detailed work on a regular basis, or who often must commit large quantities of information to memory, will find this stone to be a useful addition to his or her palette. If used on the solar plexus chakra, it encourages strength, will power, and boldness. If placed in a hot bath, it can help soothe anxiety and hysteria. It has strong yang energy, so may be inappropriate for those wishing to augment and get in touch with yin. It can deflect negative energy, and can be helpful to sufferers of jetlag, or those going through a particularly difficult time.

Marble:

This common and almost ordinary stone comes in shades of white, brown, yellow, red, green, gray, and black. Though commonplace, it is certainly a useful stone. It is useful for purifying the blood, skin, and circulatory system. If used in meditation, it can promote a state of profound stillness and awareness of the universe's vibrations. It will help the yogi or mediator gain strength self control, focus, and mastery of thought. It enhances the benefits of serenity and peace. It is a good addition to any bedroom as it helps with dream recall, provides protection, has a calming effect, and grounds the physical and emotional mind.

Meteorite:

These powerful, unassuming looking stones amplify thoughts, the reception of telepathic sending messages, greater awareness of the universe's vibrations, and connection to extraterrestrial life. Meteorites have a very usual energy that some are drawn to, but some find extremely disconcerting. As such, they are best when used by those drawn to them. Some believe that meteorites have preserved the energy of the cosmos and the upper atmosphere, and that the bearer can channel and absorb this energy. Others believe that that since they have no connection to Earth—other than falling there and burning up in the atmosphere—meteorite energy cannot be absorbed or understood by terrestrial beings.

Mochi Balls:

These strange, ironstone concretions are found at the base of the Navajo Sandstone formation, and are named after a Native American tribe from the Moqui Desert. Tribe members would use these balls in much the same manner that one could use marbles or game pieces. They also could be used in rituals for astral travel, or to prepare for psychedelic journeys. They do not need to be cleaned and are a powerful protector when placed in a room or worn as an amulet. They are a blend of male and female energy, and can help , balance the aura, realign the energy centers, relieve energy blockage, ground, center and protect. They have been used to treat constricted or collapsed veins, torn muscles, blocked arteries, immune system ailments, and osteoporosis.

Moldavite:

This moss colored stone is great for channeling good energy, especially when used on the heart chakra. It used on the crown or third eye, it can nurture telepathic abilities, and make the bearer more in tune with vibrations and messages from the earth and the universe. Those struggling to adjust to the physical world, and their current incarnation, can benefit from meditating with the stone, or using it for gazing. It helps the physical body by reducing the acuteness of asthma attacks, and dulls allergic reactions. It can help smooth out emotional intensity and prevent epileptic seizures. Some report that meditating with moldavite brings on a spacey, disconnected state, and recommend that the bearer turn to a grounding stone after using moldavite. This fragile stone should not be cleaned with salt water.

Moonstone:

This semi-precious stone is translucent with flecks of pink, purple, blue, or yellow. It is filled with yin energy, and can bring women in touch with the goddess within, and with the magic of femininity. It acts as a palliative for stress, anxiety, PMS, and cramps. It sharpens sensitivity to the emotions and energies of others while still allowing the bearer to keep in touch with the core self. If used in chakra work, it can balance energy and encourage it to gently flow. It can be used as an amulet during journeys over water. It can calm hysteria and nervousness. Moonstones are excellent for those trying to conceive, or just nurture living creatures in the home (plants, new pets, etc). If used on the brow chakra, moonstones can encourage dream recall, psychic awareness, telepathy, and intuition. At the time of the full moon or menstruation, women should be aware of their emotional state and remove these stones if it becomes necessary. They encourage fertility, and increase the robustness of the female reproductive tract. Men who wish to get in touch with their yin energy can benefit from using this stone in meditation.

Morganite/Pink Beryl:

This soft-pink or violet stone ranges from translucent to clear. It has very tender energy, and inspires open-heartedness, compassion, empathy, patience, and nurturing. It is best when used on the Heart Chakra, and can help the physical body with problems of the heart, lungs, respiratory process, and throat. Though its energy is soft, it is powerful, and excellent for those who suffer from anxiety, trust issues, or low self esteem.

Mother of Pearl

These shiny, pearl-like, multicolored beauties come from the inside of oyster shells, and as such, have a lot of ocean energy. Mother of pearl can induce relaxation, soothe tension, and alleviate stress. Moonstone is a great stone to pair with mother of pearl.

Muscovite

Also known as mica, this crystal appears in sheet-like layers or scales. It is a great stone for inspiring reflection and self-assessment. It allows one to reflect on the past and the self objectively, and without fear. It can also aid in auric cleansing, and unblocking of psychic channels. Mica encourages clarity in visions and self-reflection. It can be used during times of cleansing or fasting to help reduce hunger pangs, provide energy, relieve dehydration, and give a general boost. It can help sufferers of insomnia, night sweats, nightmares, restless leg syndrome, and sleep apnea as well.

N

Nephrite:

Nephrite looks like a creamier, more translucent version of jadeite. This stone, like jade, is thought to bring health, wealth, and longevity. It can also help those who wish for more courage, wisdom, mercy, emotional balance, stamina, fidelity, humility, generosity, and inner peace. It can benefit the physical body by toning the heart, thymus, immune system, kidneys, blood, and nervous system. Its energy is almost perfectly balanced between in and yang. It used on the brown chakra, it can help the bearer rid him or herself of negative thoughts and energy. It also the body's filtration and cleansing systems and assists in efficiently expelling toxins. It is a very protective stone and is excellent to use in amulets and stone layouts.

O

Obsidian:

Obsidian is actually lava that has been hardened in cool water. It has strong grounding properties and is an excellent protector. This stone brings about objectivity, and the opportunity for honest self-assessment. If used on the heart chakra, it absorbs and dissolves anger, criticism, bitterness, and fear, and encourages openheartedness even for the most cautious. It also has the unique ability to absorb bad vibrations and reflect them back out as white light energy. It is a warm and friendly stone, and when used on the root Chakra, has the most grounding effect. Black obsidian, when used on the root chakra, will encourage proper energy flow in the body and remove any energy blockages between the chakras. Obsidian can also be helpful for meditation and divination, and for that reason is, often found in mirrors and crystal balls. The astral travel enthusiast will also find this stone very useful. When it comes to the physical body, obsidian continues to have a lot to offer. It is able to draw imbalances to the surface and allow them to diffuse away from the body.

Obsidian is used in the area of North for personal journeys and in the Center area for grounding and protection. It is generally solid black to smoky in appearance, and has a lot of potential for variation due to the manner in which it's formed. Bubbles of air can get trapped in molten rock, which, when densely packed, cause a rainbow of colors to shine softly in the stone. When clusters of small cristobalite or feldspar get trapped in a chunk of obsidian, it appears to be flecked with snowflakes. Apache tears are the results of wind and water smoothing out the rock. When iron is introduced into the formation, mahogany obsidian is formed.

Apache Tears Infused Obsidian

Apache Tears was named in honor of the tears shed for the warriors who were driven over cliffs by the cavalry. As such, this mixture of Apache Tears and Obsidian can be used for comfort in times of grief or acute stress. This stone allows us to gain perspective while facing particularly difficult challenges, and is best used on the heart chakra.

Blue Obsidian:

This variety of obsidian encourages telepathic and verbal communication, helps with astral travel, and is good for divination and tarot reading. It can be used as an amulet to ward off negativity and is an extremely protective stone for journeys over water. It is best for facilitating communication, psychic or otherwise, when used on the throat chakra.

Green Obsidian:

This is great to pair with crystals that have lost their energies, or that are weak even after a long recharge. The green obsidian can be wrapped in silk or velvet with the ailing stone, and placed in sun or moonlight for best results. If used alone, it can balance energy flow through the heart chakra, and is good for auric cleansing or Reiki. It has slightly stronger feminine energy, and is good for encouraging nurturing, love, and gentleness.

Rainbow Obsidian:

Obsidian with ribbons of various colors can bring a full spectrum of light into one's life. Known as the "stone of pleasure", it can help open all chakras so as to accept all good energies and vibrations. It is also used for "gazing" and can be particularly useful for those seeking to further the development of the etheric and physical bodies.

Snowflake:

This obsidian stone gets the snowflake pattern on its surface from inclusions of phynocryst. This variety of obsidian is drives introspection and self-assessment, and allows us to recognize harmful patterns in our lives. It promotes self-esteem and confidence, and allows us to be more open to ambient good energy.

Strawberry Obsidian:

This rare variety of obsidian is a vibrant red, containing a lot of fire energy. It stimulates the root chakra, and encourages a noticeable uptick in vigorousness of the physical body. It also has a powerful ability to ground, and as such, can soothe or ameliorate anxiety. It has strong yang qualities, and could be good for those seeking to get in touch with masculine energy.

Violet Obsidian:

This rare stone has cooling properties, and is excellent when used on the Third Eye and crown chakras. It facilitates a connection with universal energy, and helps the bearer get in touch with universal vibrations. It is good for cleaning the auric field, and is an excellent gazing stone. Though of the earth, it contains a lot of sky and air energy.

Onyx:

This stone is good for balancing the emotions, and for grounding. It reduces the preoccupation with distractions of the physical body, such as hunger and sex drive, and absorbs and flattens negative vibrations. It is excellent for aligning the physical and spiritual bodies, and is great for divination and tarot. It promotes self-awareness and fearlessness of the unknown. It is good for the physical body in that benefits the muscle tissue, the bone marrow, the teeth, and the feet. Black: An Onyx stone will retain a spiritual imprint of its bearer, and as such, it is a good tool in psychometry because it tells the emotional and spiritual story of the wearer. As it is known for grounding and giving strength, it is a good stone for athletes or people under extreme mental and emotional stress. It brings balance to mind or body as well as strength of mind. It is highly recommended that Onyx be used in conjunction with Pearl and Diamond.

Opal:

This beautiful semi-precious gem has a lot of water energy, and a lot of ying. In meditation, it is useful amplifying and mirroring feelings, buried emotions, and repressed desires. It is excellent for visualization, imagination, dreams, and psychic healing when used on the brown and crown chakras. It should be cleansed often, but very gently, and never with salt water. Ideally it should be charged by placing it in the light of a full moon. This is an excellent gem for stone layouts if one wishes to intensify his or her emotional state, especially when paired with other stones with a lot of water energy.

Black/Dark Blue Opal:

This rare variety of opal is one of the most potent. It is an exceptionally good talisman for luck and material success.

Fire Opals:

Like all opals, this variety stirs emotions, but focuses specifically on emotions of passion. As such, they are not ideal for people combating anger management issues.

P

Pearl:

Pearls have a lot of water and lunar energy. They are extremely absorbent of thoughts and emotions so they need to be cleansed often. Otherwise, they will hold both negative and positive energy indefinitely. Pearls can cool and soothe, and are recommended for women experiencing a difficult time during pregnancy. If using pearls in conjunction with other gemstones, consider Diamonds to amplify and purify, or Emeralds to bring negative energy out and disperse it. If used on the heart and root chakras, they can stimulate the heart, and benefit the liver and the immune system. Pearls can relieve uneasiness, nervousness, anxiety and tension. Pearls promote sound sleep, prevent nerve-disorders and nerve weakness, and are commonly used to prevent or overcome fatigue. They can also have a positive effect on those prone to holding in emotions. Scuba divers, surfers, and ocean enthusiasts might consider wearing pearls as talismans against shark attacks. Older forms of Asian medicine credit pearls with the ability to relieve anxiety, to benefit reproduction, and to relieve fevers and arthritis. It was also believed that they could improve eyesight, promote muscle development and to invigorate blood circulation. Pearl powder is used topically in skin creams to purify, clean, and brighten the skin. Pearls promote the regeneration of new cells and make the skin smooth, fine, elastic and healthy. Cultivated pearls are not considered to be of the same herbal quality as natural pearls.

Pecos Diamonds:

Pecos diamonds are colorful quartz crystals that are formed inside gypsum. They settle turbulent emotions, and although they can be used with success on the heart chakra, they can be used much in the same way that worry beads or prayer beads are used. They can also be placed near a meditative place for increased tranquility during meditation and gazing. They inspire playfulness and lightheartedness, and bring a sense of calmness and peace of mind. They are also said to assist in creativity and initiation.

Peridot:

This stone can be a good overall attracter of wealth, while an adequate protector against bad energy. Peridot stones can soothe anger, fear, jealousy, and anxiety. They are good for use in divination and meditating, and can help us connect to past lives, and get in touch with the vibrations of the universe. They can assist us in visualizing our path to a state of spiritual nirvana and total stillness. The greener stones are best used on the heart chakra, and the yellowish ones on the solar plexus. They can benefit the physical body by cleaning and toning the physical heart, and strengthening the respiratory system. They encourage the release of toxins, and can neutralize those that cannot be released. They also can hasten tissue regeneration.

Petalite:

This is a very powerful protector against bad energy, negative vibrations, and even voodoo and black magic. It is said to allow the bearer to be guided by his or her angel. When used in meditation or gazing, it brings peace and stillness. It can enhance the bearer's ability to perceive psychic vibrations and the energies of other people. It is wonderful for auric cleansing, and functions well alone or with other stones.

Petrified Wood:

Petrified wood comes in a variety of shades and textures, and can benefit the circulatory, musculoskeletal, and respiratory systems. They are excellent in healing layouts, and benefit athletes tremendously because they aid in the repair of muscle damage. It can also help sufferers of arterial sclerosis, arthritis, rheumatism, dementia, and blood clots. It has strong earth energy, and is balanced between ying and yang.

Phenacite:

These stones are wonderful for healing the psychic body. They can open the third eye, crown and root Chakra as well as unblock auric cloudiness. It is excellent for sharpening skills in communication, meditation, divination, and astral travel. It can energize and empower the essence of other stones, and can be used in stone layouts by those who are more experienced with crystals. It is a powerful stone for clearing and activating the chakras, in particular, the Third Eye and Crown chakras. It can alleviate feelings of despair and fear of change, and lead one to be more conscious of the benefits of tuning into the energies of a group or community. Some pieces also contain Seraphinite, which is an excellent stone for healing and bringing positive change to one's life.

Platinum:

This is a shiny, silvery metal found in North America, Brazil, and Germany. It is rare and very expensive, and is actually so compatible with the human body's energy that it can be used in implanted or embedded medical devices. It has very cool, mellow energy, and can help keep hormones and chemical levels balanced. It is great for improving motor skills and coordination, and can help sufferers of anxiety and nervousness.

Prehnite:

This stone is wonderful for recalling dreams and past lives. It can bring calmness and balance to the heart chakra, and is excellent for gazing and meditation. Prehnites on the whiter side can aid in ensuring proper energy flow through the chakras, and it can strengthen the auric field. Great for sufferers of mononucleosis, fibromialgia, and exhaustion, it multiplies and increases energy. It is very useful for tarot, divination, and astral travel, clearing psychic channels and allowing us to increase our ability for prophesy and our harmony with the universe. It can be used in healing remedies such as crystal elixirs or solarized water, in meditation or in layout. Practitioners of reiki often find that this stone brings calm and peacefulness to any room, and as such, yoga teachers, masseuses, or therapists may wish to consider including prehnite in their work. They can strengthen the aura and balance chakra energies. Because of its effect on the Heart Chakra, it works well on the thymus gland, helps alleviates deep fears, phobias and nightmares, and can benefit kidney, bladder issues, as well as, gout and blood related disorders. Those who practice feng shui will find this a wonderful decluttering stone, and it can be placed anywhere in a room that needs balance or cleansing. Used in the Center area, however, it will best encourage grounding, balance, good health, spirituality and protection.

Pyrite/Fool's Gold:

This is an excellent grounding stone, and helps in conducting energy, invigorating the auric field, and focusing rogue energy. It can be used as a talisman for prosperity, and encourages focus, logic, and serenity. As such, it's great for sufferers of ADD, depression, hyperactivity, and anxiety. When used on the yellow chakra, it is beneficial to the stomach and intestines, soothing ulcers and making the absorption of vitamins and minerals more efficient. It also helps circulation, acidity imbalances, and GIRD. It is also excellent for the circulatory and respiratory systems. It can benefit the skin, hair, and nails as a result. It also is connected to the transfer of oxygen from the lungs to the bloodstream. Helps the skin protect itself from the elements, and also aids the digestive tract, lessening irritation caused by toxins. If used in meditation, it can also help balance creative and intuitive impulses with those that are more practical and more grounded. Communication skills, both psychic and verbal, can also improve with the help of Pyrite. Pyrite is excellent when paired with fluorite.

Q

Quartz: "Rock Crystal"

Quartz is an excellent healer. It is probably the most versatile healing stone, and is an essential addition to any crystal or stone collection. They are easy to clean and charge, and can store or amplify energy to be used in healing. Quartz can both draw and send energy therefore it is effective for telepathy, astral travel, and communication on a psychic level. Quartz is used for transformation in healing and can stimulate the auric field. It works with all chakras, and is wonderful for auric balancing, and for balancing and evening energy flow between the chakras. Quartz can be used to facilitate both speaking and receiving information from the ambient environment, gurus, teachers and healers. It stimulates positive thought and open-heartedness. It can work well when used in crystal elixirs, lunar water, or solarized water, in clusters during meditation, in reiki grids or layouts. Quartz can be placed anywhere in a space in order to balance and align its energy. It will work especially well in the center, however, and will encourage grounding, balance, good health, spirituality and protection. Quartz encompasses a large family of stones and crystals, all of which are made up primarily of silicon dioxide. Crystals of pure quartz can be found in all shades and colors. Quartz crystals grow singularly or in groups and take on different shapes according to the temperature at the time of their formation. Quartz crystals can also contain other minerals "frozen" within. Other members of the Quartz family include Chalcedony, Agate, Amethyst, Aventurine, Carnelian, Citrine, Herkimer Diamonds, Jasper, Onyx, Sardonyx and Tiger's Eye. These are treated separately because their healing qualities are very different from crystal or "rock" quartz.

Blue Quartz:

These rare stones can vary in color from pale blue to lavender or even gray. It is particularly beneficial for the chakras on the upper torso and related organs. It can help get toxins out of the bloodstream, and heightens the immunity to disease-causing imbalances. It has a calming effect, and is a good healing stone for linking the heart with Throat and Brow Chakra to expand self expression and creativity, and refine communication skills. Singers and public speakers may find it especially useful as it eases throat tension. It can help the immune system, and stimulate absorption of vitamin B. Some say shining light through Blue Quartz can be very beneficial for the eyes.

Clear Quartz:

Clear quartz amplifies energy levels in the auric field, and can invigorate the physical body. It can assist in the creation of power, clarity of thinking, meditation, cleansing, clearing the aura, spiritual development and healing. It is excellent for those seeking more self esteem, or more confidence. Pure white light passes through it easily, leaving all the colors of the spectrum unaltered, and is excellent in stone layouts. They can amplify whatever influences are present in the bearer or space. They can tune into the frequencies of each individual, and will retain a "psychic fingerprint" of its bearer unless cleansed. Clear Quartz can be cleansed with spring water, and charged with solar energy, lunar energy, or the energy of the bearer fairly easily. If used on the brow chakra, it unblocks specific areas or organs blocked from transmitting or receiving the flow of energy throughout the body. It aids in meditation and can be used well with other stones. It will amplify the effects of individual stones and attune the treatment to the energy of an individual person.

Dendritic Quartz:

This quartz is excellent for divination, as it has shapes on its surface that can resemble plants or animals. Elestial crystals are crystals that generally have fewer side planes and blunt ends. These crystals are young and usually much smaller than most other Quartz crystals. They are wonderful for gazing and auric cleansing. They work well with other stones, and can be charged with lunar or solar energy easily.

Harlequin Quartz:

This is a unique blend of two minerals and can be used for balance, energy and vitality. Their energy is distinct and fluid, and if the bearer can tune into it, energy flow will be stimulated on all levels, and the auric field will be made more vibrant. Harlequins contain red dots or strands of hematite or lepidocrocite. As such, they combine the properties of quartz with hematite or lepidocrocite, both of which are excellent for giving energy to the physical body, and stimulating circulation. It can be used with good results on the Root chakra and to provide for a direct pathway between the base chakra and the heart chakra, clearing paths blocking the flow of energy throughout the chakras. It activates all the qualities of the Root chakra, the heart chakra, and the crown chakra, and stimulates the healing qualities of the heart.

Purple Quartz:

This stone can be easily mistaken for amethyst, but it has very different properties. It has a dark violet color and may have inclusions or clouding within it. They are excellent for aiding in the elimination of toxins, stimulating the immune system, and strengthening the cleansing organs. They benefit the skin, hair, and nails. They are not the best stone to use in meditation or gazing, as they palpably stimulate thoughts and brain activity, and encourage analysis and contemplation.

Single and Double-Terminated Clear Quartz:

Single-terminated Clear Quartz crystals are six-sided with a flat bottom and point at the top. They are excellent for focusing rogue or scattered energy, and are a great meditative tool for those wishing to pinpoint their efforts on healing a specific organ or area on the body. Double-terminated Clear Quartz crystals are very rare. Most terminated crystals grow out of rock, often in clusters with other crystals. Double-terminated Clear Quartz crystals grow in clay or other soft materials, and are pointed on both ends. As such, they can act as a magnet, and can draw energy as well as direct it. The center of the crystal works like a neutralizing chamber to sap the strength out of bad energy. One of the points acts as a magnet to negative vibrations and negative energy. The energy is collected and directed into the center of the crystal, where it is transformed and purified. The now-positive energy then passes out of the crystal through the other point.

Tangerine Quartz:

This vibrant variety of quartz comes from Madagascar.

They are quartz crystals with a transparent coating of bright orange over them. Orange is the color of the second chakra, which has to do with the reproductive organs and creativity. The energy of Tangerine quartz is bright, lively, and sparkling. Anyone who wishes to open, massage, or activate a blocked or unresponsive Navel Chakra would benefit from working with this stone. As they are long crystals, they could be used as wands. They are also an excellent addition to stone layouts.

R

Rose Quartz:

Rose quartz encourages love, tranquility, peacefulness, openheartedness, and generosity. Rose Quartz works with the heart chakra, and emits a soft, gentle, soothing energy that warms the heart center. It can be used with excellent results in meditation, and can soothe sufferers of insomnia, anxiety, schizophrenia, PTSD, and heartbreak. It can also diffuse negative stimuli and uncomfortable memories. It opens the heart chakra in that it encourages us to not only understand and love others, but to understand and love ourselves. It is of particular value in helping us to forgive ourselves, hastening self-acceptance. It opens channels of psychic empathy and communication. Rose Quartz can be used to facilitate emotional healing, ease loss, calm stress, relieve hurt, dissolve fear, help strengthen low confidence, and diffuse anger. It can be a valuable tool in a therapist's arsenal, giving comfort to people working through difficult or traumatic issues. Rose quartz can also be a good tool in chakra and auric work. It can also align mental, emotional, and astral bodies, and can make sure that energy flows through the chakras. It benefits the physical body in that it can act as a palliative towards inflammation and fever. It stimulates the cleansing organs and the skin. The reproductive organs may become healthier and fertility can

increase. It is also excellent in gem layouts. It does,
however, need to be recharged and cleansed often. Rose
Quartz can be used to balance both Yin and Yang. Placing
rose quartz in the center of a room or space can help
dissipate negative or erratic energy.

Rhodochrosite:

This stone has a very vibrant energy that locks in with the
heart chakra, removing blockages that prevent the bearer
from giving or receiving positive energy. Rhodochrosite has
been referred to as the best stone for encouraging love and
balance. It is excellent to stave off loneliness and
heartache, and is a good tool to use in meditation for those
seeking to combat emotional damage caused by PTSD,
fear, insecurities, inner-child issues, abuse, or neglect. It
can be worn for 24 hours straight before it will have to be
recharged or cleansed. It is an excellent talisman for good
energy, and is a superior choice for those who wish to
bolster self esteem and ability to trust. It can also be used
in times of change or transition by providing comfort and
support. It is also good for encouraging restful, peaceful
sleep with pleasant dreams.

Though it works well with the heart chakra, this crystal is
also recommended for use with the solar plexus, where it

will benefit those with food issues, food addictions, anorexia, and metabolism problems. It can also benefit the physical body by helping unsettled stomachs, and can be used to detoxify the blood and the liver. If placed in a hot bath, it will invigorate the bather. This is also good for the respiratory system, and is wonderful for sufferers of asthma, bronchitis, or tracheitis. It can work well with other stones, but is complemented especially well by malachite and copper.

This stone can come in shades of orange and pink. It often has stripes of various widths in shades of white.

Rhodonite:

Rhodonite works well with the heart chakra, soothing the heart center and opening blocked energy channels. It also does well with the root chakra, where it can ground and balance. The black oxides in the stone allows for the stimulation of self worth and self love. Caution should be used, however, because it can work so well as to inspire selfishness and arrogance. When used properly and in the right amounts, it can help us express confidence and lovingness on the physical plane via physical and emotional means. It calms and feeds the aura through the heart. It is excellent for use in meditation, yoga, chanting, affirmation, mantras, and reiki. It can help strengthen and focus dedication, commitment, and resolve during all of the above activities. Rhodonite can also be used to alleviate anxiety and heartache, and stimulate self reflection and honest self assessment. It can benefit the physical body by strengthening the teeth, nails, and bones. If placed in the center of a room or space, rhodonite can encourage emotional and spiritual balance, and can ground the energy in the room. It is generally pink, with black inclusions.

Rhyolite:

Rhyolite is a striking stone, with beautiful bands, bubbles and layers that form as lava flows onto the surface of stone and moves forward. Because of the way it is formed, the shape, size, and exact color of rhyolite can vary greatly. It is composed of the light-colored silicates and is usually buff to pink in color. It represents change, growth, diversity, and progress. It can be used to inspire creativity, dedication, drive, and a willingness to seek change and move forward. It gives the bearer an increased tolerance for change, instability, growth, and the unfamiliar. It encourages tolerance, understanding, and a thirst for knowledge. It can bring excellent results in meditation and gazing.

Ruby:

This red stone intensifies the emotions and stokes passions. It can be used as a talisman to bring wealth, joy, love, sexual vigor, and power. It can warm and energize even the most sluggish aura, and as such, is excellent for the convalescing or infirmed. It can strengthen and energize both the physical heart and the heart chakra, opening blocked channels so that the bearer can better send and receive love, courage, confidence, vitality, stamina, strength, leadership, and success. If used on the root chakra, it can act as an aphrodisiac and encourages the bearer to get in touch with the condition and needs of the physical body. It can also help heal infections, lower cholesterol, resolve blood clots, detoxify the blood, and ease the difficulties associated with going sober. It stimulates circulation, menses, and the pituitary gland. Because it is so invigorating and the energy is so strong, rubies must be selected carefully, and discarded if the energy is wrong. The stone is usually a deep, brilliant red, but can be found shades of pink or lavender. It is an amplifier of energy-both positive and negative, so it should be used with care. It has a lot of yang energy, and can bring anger or negativity to the surface quickly. For this reason, it may not be the ideal stone for the hyperactive, or those afflicted with ADD or profound anxiety. It greatly benefits the heart and circulatory system, and can assist in the filtration and detoxification of waste in the body.

Rutilated/Rutile Quartz:

This is clear quartz with bands of golden rutile, copper, or blue/gray titanium fibers. These other stones and materials can conduct and amplify energy, thoughts, and vibrations. Using these stones in meditation can hasten the onset of a trance-like state. These stones are also very useful for opening the Crown Chakra for meditation, clairvoyance, telepathy, and psychic communication. The golden fibers may increase radiation protection, and encourage swifter cellular regeneration. Each stone has its own unique energy, and as such, stones should be personally and carefully selected.

S

Sapphire:

These lovely semi-precious stones can be blue, green, pink, purple, or clear. The blue varieties can work well to stimulate communication, insight, intuition, divination, inspiration, and stillness. Blue is also good for stimulating the pituitary gland and the thyroid. It can also work to detox the skin and invigorate the auric field. The energy is very cooling, and as such, it can reduce infection, inflammation, fevers, and nosebleeds. Some also report good results in using blue sapphires to heal burns. If used to cleanse the auric field, it can also benefit the nervous system and meridians. For best results, wear sapphires directly on the skin, particularly if wearing it close to the throat chakra. Using sapphires in meditation can encourage wisdom, will, centering, cheerfulness, and general good luck. Some report success in using sapphire to palliate the effects of radiation and to soothe anxiety. Dark sapphires are more grounding, and offer more protection against negative energies. Darker sapphires are also excellent for alleviating tension and for aligning the mental, physical, and spiritual planes. This can be an excellent stone for people with spiritual confusion or depression, or those feeling as though they are trapped in a situation that is beyond their control.

Star Sapphire:

These are very similar to blue sapphires; however, they have inclusions in their makeup that creates a refracted five-pointed star on the stone's surface. This star is a focus point in the gem and is excellent for focusing and grounding energy. Star sapphires are recommended for people who wish to awaken or heighten their psychic abilities, and improve their abilities to tune into ambient vibrations. They are also good for gazing and meditation, and can function as a relaxing agent during times of extreme physical exertion. Healers of the spirit and body are often drawn to this stone, and it can be a good tool in the arsenal of reiki practitioners.

Sard:

This is a rather ordinary looking brick-red stone. It is not generally considered to be a strong healer, though it does possess limited properties similar to Carnelians. It has been suggested that these stones are good for healing open wounds and resolving conditions of the blood. Sard can also be beneficial to the cleansing organs and in strengthening to the mind during times of stress or weakened resolve.

Sardonyx:

This stone is actually a layered combination of Sard and Onyx. As such, its appearance can vary greatly, and can include shades of red, brown, black or white. They are especially beneficial for the cardiopulmonary systems. They can also be good for helping sufferers of depression, or for the bipolar. Red stones stimulate and invigorate, brown grounds and centers, black absorbs, and white acts to detoxify and purify. The colors do not cancel each other out. They do, however, buffer each other and maintain a median balance that allows the bearer to affect change and benefit. They may be most useful for explorers, martial artists, and executives.

Selenite:

Selenite been used to accelerate the expulsion and remission of cancer and can stabilize epileptic disorders. Selenite also encourages mental and emotional focus, growth, luck, and immunity from disease. This is an excellent tool for gazing or for meditation,. As it smoothes emotions and focuses scattered or misfired energy waves. Holding the crystal and visualizing it bringing white light from the transpersonal point above head down through body, and out through the feet, can energize all of the chakras and stimulate energy flow through them. This practice can benefit those feeling sluggish, or out of tune with ambient vibrations or energies. It can also be placed on the third eye chakra to open it. It can also benefit the physical body by strengthening the spine and nerve system, and encouraging agility and flexibility. It can greatly heighten sensitivity to others' auric fields, and stimulate telepathic abilities.

Desert Rose

This beautiful form of selenite forms clusters like rose buds, and are excellent for lactating mothers. They encourage lactation, and soothe discomforts associated with breastfeeding. They work on all chakras but are especially useful when used on the heart chakra. They are a good stone to have in spaces reserved for tai chi, yoga, or meditation as they infuse a space with gentle, warm energy.

Serpentine:

This stone is an excellent stone for gazing and for meditation. It can be used to clear clouded areas of all of the chakras, and is especially effective when used to open the heart chakra. It is also believed to help activate the kundalini energies, and can invigorate spaces for yoga or Tai chi. Using this stone on the crown chakra can initiate movement of kundilini energy up the spine, and through the chakras.

Serpentine emits a profound healing vibration and facilitates the activation of cellular regeneration, even in the brain. The stone can offer assistance to the immune system in its endeavor to heal disorders in all areas of the body, the emotional system, and brain. It benefits the heart and lungs by helping to draw out toxins and activate the absorption of nutrients and oxygen. It is frequently used in the treatment of diabetes and hypoglycemia. It also kills parasites and used to increase the absorption of magnesium and calcium.

This stone is light to dark green to whitish green in color and its surface can take on an appearance that looks like snakeskin. It can yield great protective abilities when worn as an amulet to protect from snakebites.

Shiva Lingham:

These stones can only be collected from the river bed of the Narmada River in the central western part of India. The river is considered a holy site. Lord Shiva is the supreme being revered by Hindus, and this fertility stone is often worshipped as his effigy or physical manifestation on earth. It generally is found in an egg-like shape, and has a glossy, smooth surface. Lingam is the Sanskrit word for phallus. This stone is excellent when used on the heart chakra, inspiring harmony and balance of the spiritual body and the auric field.

Silica: "Gem Silica"

The highest, purest form of gem quality Chrysocolla. This is an excellent blue green stone, and it has lots of water and yin energy.

Silver:

This is an excellent metal for mental, emotional, and physical releasing and cleansing. It encourages balance and grounding. Like the moon's energy, it has a gentle, cool, smoothing effect, acting to benefit the physical body by reducing fever, inflammation, and nervous system stress. It can work well alone but it also gives good results when paired with blue or green gems. It stimulates the pituitary glands and massages the upper energy centers, as well as the upper chakras. Because this metal has so much potential and is so powerful, it is important that you select the silver yourself to make sure it is the best for your energy.

Silver also encourages both verbal and psychic communication, and it can be work all the time if desired. In addition to encouraging good energy flow between the chakras, it can help the physical body by stimulating efficient blood circulation, and detoxifying the blood. This in turn benefits sufferers of degenerative brain disease, poor memory, irrational fears, and emotional imbalance. Silver can also help the bearer become aware of chemical or emotional imbalances so that they become corrected sooner than later. Silver also can soothe respiratory organs that have been damaged or irritated by secondhand smoke or other pollutants. If worn below the navel, as a belly ring or a belt buckle, for instance, it can stimulate the reproductive organs and increase fertility. It can also help resolve sexual problems that result from dysfunction or impotence. Wearing silver close to the head, such as in earrings or a necklace, can increase overall mental functioning, and lessen anxiety associated with decision making.

The best results will come by pairing it with Agate, Jet, Moonstone, and Turquoise.

Smithsonite:

This stone comes in shades of light blue, or light pink, and can appear to be infused with little bubbles. It has the ability to harmonize and align the heart, throat, and brow chakra, enabling better communication, more effective leadership, and improved perceptiveness. If used in meditation or in a meditative space, the bearer will find that he or she is given more clarity. It can also assist in past lives recall, divination, and dream interpretation. It works to stimulate the heart chakra, and benefits the sense of smell, the lymph nodes, and the immune system. Some also say that it increases tissue elasticity.

Smoky Quartz:

This is a very versatile stone, and can help with depression, anxiety, and epilepsy. Smoky quartz crystals can vary in appearance, but can be root beer, grayish, or chocolate-colored clear crystals. The clearest in color are usually the best for opening the crown chakra, and can clear blocked channels of energy throughout the chakras. Use in gazing or meditation can also produce good results, facilitating the perception of ambient vibrations and energies. They can also be used to stimulate meridians, encourage kundalini energy, and correct imbalances that cause infertility, PMS, and other reproductive problems.

These stones are also excellent at absorbing energy, and as such, should be cleaned fairly regularly. They can alleviate fear, anxiety, and depression. The browner shades can be very grounding, but sometimes are so saturated with grounding energy that they feel dense, or impermeable and incapable of conducting anything. All colors and varieties of this stone are useful for correcting problems in the lower torso, including digestive and sexual problems. The stone can benefit both sexes in this respect. Some say that the smoky quality of this quartz is a result of radiation, so the utmost care should be used when working with smoky quartz.

Sodalite:

This is a good stone for use in reiki and meditation work. It is also a good, all purpose tool for encouraging verbal and psychic communication. Its connection with the throat chakra means that it can also soothe irritated or inflamed respiratory organs. Sodalite can also be very effective when used at the brow chakra, and will assist the bearer in tuning into ambient energy waves. Those who need to fine tune telepathic, psychic, and intuitive abilities may wish to use this stone in such a capacity. The stone can also encourage camaraderie with others, and benefit a community as a whole when placed in a common or often trafficked space. Using the stone for gazing can also help the bearer engage in honest self-assessment and self-analysis, gently guiding him or her to find the right balance between the desire for self improvement and the desire for self acceptance. The stone benefits the physical body by balancing energy levels in the thyroid, pituitary gland, and lymph nodes. Use of the stone on a regular basis can have salubrious effects on insomnia and restless leg syndrome. This stone is cooling and is used for drawing out infections, cooling burns, healing sinus inflammation, breaking up congestion, and reversing high blood pressure. It is also valuable because it is helpful in balancing the metabolism. It furthermore tones the cleansing organs and can stimulate the immune system. It acts as a barrier against natural and artificial radiation and is recommended for those who work around X-ray equipment or are involved with radioactive material. This stone's Latin name is said to mean "a cure for headaches".

Spinel:

This stone, which can sometimes be mistaken for a ruby, comes in shades of red, blue, or green. It is a very soothing stone, and calms and alleviates stress, anxiety, PTSD, and depression. It is also good for basic mental invigoration and rejuvenation. When used to benefit the physical body, it is most commonly used to aid in detoxification, as a partner with fasting, enemas, natural diuretics, and natural cleansing teas. It can benefit the skin and the hair as well. The red varieties of the stone can also be used to encourage spiritual strength. Spinels are most commonly found in the US, USSR, Sri Lanka, Italy, and Germany. It can encourage moderation of all excesses—including food and sleep--and aid in the detoxification of both the blood and the mind. ☐

Star Ruby:

This stone is said to promote lucid dreaming and can to clear channels of communication between the self and spirit guides. It can be used as a conductor of energy, and can clear a pathway between the user to electrical and magnetic forces. It assists in purifying, and correcting rogue energy which can lead to atrophy of the auric field. It helps to align the auric, spiritual, and physical bodies as one. It is an excellent stone for releasing blocks to accepting and giving energy. Star Ruby is a stone of great energy, development and protection. It releases negative energy and serves as a tool of empowerment. It helps in the focus of healing energies and clearing pathways. □

Staurolite:

Also referred to a fairy cross, this mineral can act as a very powerful magnet for general good luck and material prosperity. This beautiful and rare stone crystallizes in the form of flat and short crystals. These twinnings of crystals occur frequently at right angles to create a shape much like a crucifix.

The stone can wield a calming, peaceful influence on a meditation space. It can also give the bearer a sense of the same calmness if worn as a pendant around the neck or simply carried in a purse or a pocket. It has the energy of all four elements and can assist the spirit in feeling harmony with the earth and its matter. It promotes spirituality, compassion, and clears pathways to receive ambient vibrations. It is also excellent for protection and grounding, and as such, works wonders on the root chakra.

Some also say that this stone can provide a connection between the physical, astral and extra-terrestrial planes. It can encourage the bearer to center him or herself during times of acute stress or chaos, and offers support, initiation and incentive in dealing with destructive habits, such as overeating and oversleeping. Used for addiction, especially for those who wish to cease and desist smoking or cocaine, the stone will ease the detoxification experience and provide support during times when it is particularly difficult to abstain. It can be used to draw out fever, soothe inflammation, and calm anxiety.

If placed in the center of a room, it can bring soothing energy and have a grounding affect.

Stichtite:

Stichtite is usually found as a deposit in or on another mineral, usually too thin or sparse to be extracted to make a pure stichtite stone of any consequential size. Stichtite is formed when continental plates collide. It can bring the bearer in tune with inner emotions and help sort out which emotions are paired with which cognitions to produce certain behaviors. In the home, it creates a tranquil environment, and can be useful in children's play rooms or common spaces where children are expected to play somewhat quietly. When used in chakra work, stichtite can ease the passage of Kundalini energy through the Heart chakra, and encourage energy to flow properly through the chakras, particularly the upper ones.

Stilbite:

This stone comes in shades of pale pink, grey, or white. Pink is especially helpful for encouraging the bearer to be open to both giving and receiving positive energy, and is especially useful for those with issues pertaining to trust and forgiveness. The stone can also be aid in detoxification.

Sugilite: "Lavulite/Royal Azele"

This stone can help enhance psychic and telemetric abilities. It can get the bearer in touch with spiritual guides. It can protect, absorb, and dissolve anger, hurt, and various negative energies. Sugilite brings white light into the physical body and heart for healing, especially when placed on the third eye chakra. It can also help to alleviate symptoms of depression, bipolar disorder, PTSD, and general listlessness. Its energy is considered androgynous but if paired with stones that have particularly strong feminine or masculine energies, it can still work well. The more purple varieties help to balance right and left brain function. It can be very helpful for easing a transition into a new environment or situation.

Sugilite can also benefit the physical body if used to draw out pain from headaches, arthritis, and carpal tunnel. It can also alleviate inflammation, stress, disease, and effects of toxins. It can balance the adrenal, pineal, and pituitary glands, and properly balance the metabolism.

Sulphur:

Sulphur can be a very useful stone for rejuvenating and healing. It comes in various shades of yellow and can be clear or opaque. It can rejuvenate both the mind and the body, and may be of special usefulness for those that work in manual labor, or are forced to concentrate for long periods of time. It may also benefit sufferers of ADD or ADHD as it encourages clarity, focus, willpower, discipline, and confidence. It can benefit the physical body if used in hot springs or hot baths for arthritis, pain, rheumatism, swelling, inflammation, problems with lymph nodes, cysts, hemorrhoids. Traditionally very healing for wounds, cleansing and healing skin, drawing out inflammation of the sinus tissue, soothing an irritated pancreas, toning the liver, ameliorating the affect of syphilis, bringing the swelling down on an irritated appendix, and calming an acidic stomach. It can also strengthen the endocrine glands. It can also act as a natural repellent for bugs.

Sunstone:

This stone has a very masculine energy, and is good for invigoration and empowerment. It can warm the heart chakra and stimulate energy flow through the auric field. It can be useful as a protective amulet, and is very grounding.

T

Tanzanite:

This rare, purple or blue stone is excellent for healing and meditation. If used in chakra work, it can open the brow and crown centers for fine-tuning skills in divination, past lives recall, and ability to tune into ambient vibrations and energy. It can greatly expand our physical and mental senses, even sharpening our sensitivity to touch. It was first discovered in Tanzania. This stone stimulates both the throat chakra and the third Eye chakra, and can encourage and improve abilities in all forms of mental and verbal communication. Tanzanite has also had good results in helping to treat depression and bipolar disorder.

Tektite:

Tektite is a type of natural glass, only found on earth within a certain specific latitude. Tektites usually have a heavily mottled surface, and are black with some golden tinge when held to the light. It can be very useful in balancing yin and yang energies, and can strengthen one's auric field.

Tiger's Eye:

This stone has a wide range of useful applications. It can act as a talisman for general courage, and luck. It can also aid the bearer in developing better communication skills, both verbal and non-verbal. It activates the solar plexus and crown chakras, and can help the bearer sort out the differences between emotions and cognitions. It also has some grounding properties, and can help the bearer become more centered, especially in times of emotional chaos. It can also help the bearer discover a balance between the drive to improve and the drive to accept. Tiger's eye works well when used with pearl or mother of pearl. Even if used alone, it can alleviate anxiety associated with decision making. Some say that it can act as a talisman for help, sending the bearer kind people who are in his or her path for a purpose.

It can benefit the physical body by helping to treat digestion and stomach disorders such as GIRD, ulcers, and acid reflux. It can also strengthen bones and assist in their proper alignment. Rubbing the stone with essential oil and using it on the solar plexus will help with detoxification of both the physical and mental bodies. It is balanced between yin and yang, and will benefit both sexes.

Topaz:

Topaz can be an excellent talisman for material wealth, and is also a good stone for correcting disorders in the physical body. The stones open the heart chakra and can open pathways of energy while still allowing the chakras to absorb energy at their own pace. The particularly sensitive may, as such, find this a particularly powerful stone for use during chakra work, as it doesn't allow the spiritual body to become overwhelmed. It also can be good for gazing as it aids in visualization skills.

Topaz most commonly is found in a brilliant yellow color, but can also be found in shades of green, blue, and brown. It is usually mined in the US, Mexico, Brazil, and Sri Lanka. It can send out energy and motivate those suffering from listlessness and sluggishness, and as such, is a useful stone for sufferers of depression, and for competitive athletes. Topaz can also stimulate the auric field, and harness rogue energy waves.

Golden or pink/"Champagne" Crystal:

This gem is among the best for activating the solar plexus chakra. It emits a strong, steady, pulsing energy, and encourages focus, concentration, determination, and stamina. It can help PMS, bipolar disorder, insomnia, depression, anxiety, mood swings, and hypoglycemic energy crashes.

It benefits the physical body by detoxifying the liver and the pancreas, balancing the blood sugar, strengthening muscle tissue, and strengthening the spinal column. It radiates warm energy, and is excellent for water signs.

Tourmaline:

This striated gem has very powerful energy. It can strengthen the body and spirit align the chakras, and allow the aura to absorb white light and positive energy. If worn as an amulet, it gives light protection to the wearer. When used in chakra work, it can benefit the nervous system.

Black Tourmaline:

Black tourmaline, contrary to what may be intuitive, repels rather than absorbs black light and negative energy. It can be an excellent amulet, and is valuable stone for crises and for periods of acute stress. It strengthens weakened immune systems, and can speed the healing process, as well as encourage tissue regeneration.

Brown Tourmaline: (Dravite) :

This variety of tourmaline is an excellent stone to use during meditation or yoga. It is said to bring a realization of the lotus within all of us. It protects the bearer from the effects of bad karma, and is very gentle for use in grounding. When used in chakra work, it can balance the chakras, cleanse the aura, and bring a warm sense of calmness to the bearer.

Tourmalinated Quartz:

Tourmalinated quartz can occur alone, or can be found embedded in Clear Quartz. This useful stone can provide a calm atmosphere useful for problem solving. It can help balance alignment between the physical and spiritual bodies, energize the chakras, and invigorate the auric field.

Turquoise:

This vibrantly colored blue or blue green stone is a wonderful all purpose healer for ailments of the physical body, and also acts as a good conductor of energy. If used on the throat chakra, it can encourage good verbal communication, and gently open the throat chakra to open the channels of spiritual and vibrational communication as well. It can also open the Heart Chakra and clear blocked pathways. If used on the brow, it can facilitate greater ability to be in tune with ambient energy and vibrations. It is extremely versatile as it aligns all meridians, chakras, and energy fields. Like amethyst, it helps correct damage caused by alcohol, pollution, radiation, drugs, and food born toxins. It is an excellent sponge for negativity.

It can help alleviate and heal headaches, throat inflammation, lung damage, asthma, infections, cavities, TMJ, tinnitus, high blood pressure, and depression. It works best with silver, although it can be paired with other stones. It is balanced between feminine and masculine energy. It should be handled with care, as turquoise can fade in sunlight and sustain damage if harsh cleaning agents are used with it.

U

Ulexite:

This white or translucent stone helps one balance the need
to prioritize the self with the need to prioritize others. It
has mixed results with 3rd eye opening, and some find it
helpful for amplifying dreams, imagination, and past lives
recall. It is necessary to be very careful when cleaning this
stone. It should be handled with care as it is very delicate,
and never washed with saline water or left to soak for too
long. It can just as well be cleansed with moonlight or solar
energy.

Unakite:

Unakite is certainly useful for soothing tension in the heart
chakra, but it also release emotions and stress stored in the
solar plexus and digestive system. When used in
meditation, unakite can encourage proper breathing so as
to facilitate proper energy flow through the chakras and
the physical body. It can also be very helpful in the steady
release of emotions that have been held in. The stone can
be a shade of opaque coral or olive-green, and actually
consists of three minerals: feldspar, epidote, and quartz.
The crystals retain their original properties in addition to

blending together and working in unison. Unakite facilitates self awareness, self assessment, and self analysis. It can be useful for healing ailments caused by stress, or other psychosomatic means.

V

Variscite:

These stones come in shades of pale green, and emanate a soothing, cooling, feminine energy. They ease depression, fear, worry, anxiety, impatience, and general stress. Using them in a bath can greatly mitigate the stress of the day by bringing calm and stillness to even the most active mind, and as such, it can also be a good stone for meditation or gazing. It can also be a good addition to a yoga studio or any space designated for meditation and healing. It can ease the difficulties associated with learning astral travel, and can soothe and even out the aura. If used on the Solar Plexus and Heart Chakra it can slow overly aggressive energy currents through the chakras, and can also somewhat benefit divination and intuition. As for the physical body, variscite encourages skin and blood vessel elasticity, and can benefit men suffering from impotence or other reproductive ailments.

W

Watermelon Quartz:

This multicolored stone is excellent for infusing a space with soft, gentle, good energy. The stones with more red in them have more grounding capabilities. Those with more pink are best for encouraging the unblocking of channels of communication, and the greener varieties excel at healing the immune system. Overall, the stone is good for balancing the metabolism, toning the endocrine system, and clearing blocked communication pathways.

Wulfenite:

This stone comes in shades of translucent yellow, orange, and red, but is usually found in some shade of orange. It invigorates and balances the emotions, passions, and the appetite. It has a very warm energy that is also grounding. It is also extremely beneficial for women who suffer from cramps on a monthly basis. If used on the navel chakra, it can stimulate the spleen and yellow chakras, and aid in digestion and the absorption of vitamins.

Z

Zebra Stone:

These distinctive looking stones are generally striped with black and white. They are excellent for managing pain in the physical body, and encourage stillness and emotional tranquility.

Zircon:

Zircon can come in all colors but it is most often clear, and is easily mistaken for a diamond by untrained eyes. Zircon can work with the Crown Chakra and strengthens intuitive abilities, emotional steadfastedness, and connections with ambient energy. It can ease depression, insomnia, and anxiety. It can be natural or human made. The natural zircon has much stronger energy than the man made variety.

Zoisite:

This green and black stone sometimes has ribbons of ruby in it. Zoisite encourages trust in the universe, and releases fears of the unknown. When used on the heart chakra, it promotes good flow of energy throughout the chakras, and strengthens the aura. As far as the physical body is concerned, it's good for overall energy levels, helping those prone to laziness and idleness. Some also say that it is beneficial to the heart, spleen, stomach, pancreas and lungs.

Index

Abalone 13
abuse 39, 69, 74, 145
acid reflux 40, 175
ADD34, 47, 100, 134, 149,
171
ADHD........... 34, 100, 171
affirmation 53, 146
Agate 13, 14, 15, 16, 17,
137, 161
air 15, 94, 106, 121, 124
Albite...........................19
Alexandrite...................19
alignment. 53, 71, 76, 175,
180
Amazonite 20
Amber......................... 20
Amethyst........ 21, 22, 137
Ammonite 24
amulet .. 13, 27, 31, 35, 51,
57, 60, 83, 94, 95, 99,
107, 112, 115, 122, 158,
172, 178, 179
amulets................. 24, 118
Angelite 24, 25
anger ...23, 25, 27, 32, 49,
60, 64, 79, 92, 106,
120, 126, 129, 143, 149,
170
animals...........25, 88, 139
anxiety.. 14, 15, 16, 21, 22,
24, 25, 31, 35, 39, 41,
48, 57, 62, 66, 71, 79,
82, 87, 92, 97, 101, 102,
103, 104, 109, 115, 116,
124, 127, 129, 132, 134,
143, 146, 149, 151, 161,

162, 163, 166, 168, 175,
178, 184, 188
Apache Tears........ 27, 121
Apatite......................... 28
aphrodisiac......16, 36, 78,
148
Apophylite.................. 29
appetite control........... 25
Aqua Aura 31
Aquamarine 33, 34, 68
Aragonite..................... 34
arthritis46, 54, 59, 61, 72,
78, 127, 130, 170, 171
Arthritis........................15
artists 20, 154
astral projection.....17, 46
Aventurine 35, 36, 137
Azurite.......... 37, 107, 108
Barite........................... 39
Barium 39
Bathing....................... 3, 9
Beryl 39, 115
bitterness 37, 49, 120
blood ... 18, 25, 28, 41, 43,
47, 50, 51, 52, 54, 60,
61, 62, 64, 65, 70, 75,
77, 79, 90, 94, 95, 102,
105, 111, 118, 128, 130,
133, 145, 148, 153, 160,
164, 166, 178, 181, 184
Bloodstone 41
Blue Lace......................14
Boji Stones 42
bones..38, 40, 44, 46, 50,
61, 71, 77, 87, 88, 146,
175

brain.. 35, 52, 64, 74, 107, 141, 157, 160, 170
Brass............................ 43
breastfeeding........50, 155
brow 37, 115, 139, 161, 164, 173, 181
bury..............................10
Calcite 44, 46, 59
calm 14, 17, 34, 41, 57, 79, 115, 133, 143, 168, 180, 184
calmness 22, 48, 128, 132, 167, 180
Carnelian........ 46, 47, 137
Celestite...................... 48
centering 14, 16, 17, 23, 24, 35, 84, 151
Cerussite 48
chakra...4, 5, 14, 15, 16, 17, 19, 20, 21, 24, 25, 27, 28, 31, 33, 35, 37, 40, 41, 46, 47, 48, 49, 52, 54, 56, 57, 59, 61, 65, 66, 69, 72, 74, 75, 79, 84, 85, 86, 87, 88, 90, 92, 94, 95, 98, 99, 100, 101, 104, 106, 109, 114, 115, 118, 120, 122, 123, 128, 129, 132, 134, 139, 140, 142, 143, 144, 145, 146, 148, 151, 155, 157, 159, 161, 162, 163, 168, 169, 170, 172, 173, 177, 178, 180, 181, 182, 186, 189
Chakra.. 14, 17, 21, 22, 25, 27, 28, 29, 33, 37, 57, 62, 69, 81, 90, 96, 116, 120, 131, 133, 138, 142, 149, 181, 184, 188

Chalcedony...........50, 137
chaos 22, 168, 175
charge............... 7, 10, 136
charisma...................... 20
Charoite.................50, 51
Chiastolite 52
childbirth 21, 24, 85
Chinese Writing Stone 53
Chrysocolla...........54, 159
Chrysoprase 56
circulatory system. 22, 61, 69, 72, 76, 79, 93, 95, 111, 149
Citrine 56, 57, 137
clairvoyance 29, 149
clarity . 22, 24, 44, 56, 69, 77, 81, 84, 117, 138, 162, 171
clean 7, 41, 128, 136
cleansing organs .. 22, 58, 95, 140, 144, 153, 164
colon............................14
comforting...................15
common sense......... 5, 22
communication 19, 20, 25, 28, 31, 33, 37, 39, 40, 62, 64, 81, 86, 96, 100, 122, 131, 136, 138, 143, 149, 151, 160, 161, 163, 166, 173, 175, 181, 186
compassion 59, 78, 99, 116, 168
confidence 20, 25, 48, 56, 64, 107, 123, 138, 143, 146, 148, 171
confusion.............. 22, 152
coordination...49, 64, 132
Copper............59, 60, 107
Coral............... 60, 61, 62

courage33, 39, 69, 76, 90, 95, 96, 118, 148, 175
Creedite 64
criticism 57, 120
crown... 37, 40, 46, 49, 51, 56, 57, 61, 66, 74, 88, 98, 99, 114, 124, 126, 131, 140, 157, 162, 173, 175
Crown 22, 57, 131, 149, 188
Crystal 28, 136, 177
Cuprite 65
Danburite 66
dealing with change 15
depression. 19, 40, 41, 47, 56, 57, 66, 71, 75, 97, 99, 103, 104, 106, 134, 152, 154, 162, 163, 166, 170, 173, 177, 178, 181, 184, 188
Desert Rose 66, 155
detoxification .. 21, 46, 51, 64, 90, 149, 166, 168, 170, 176
Diamond 68, 125
diets 21
Diopside 68
Dioptase 69
diseases 18, 54, 72, 77, 93
divination .. 17, 75, 86, 99, 100, 120, 122, 125, 129, 131, 132, 139, 151, 162, 173, 184
Dolomite 71
dream .. 21, 29, 39, 44, 53, 85, 99, 100, 111, 115, 162
dream recall 21, 29, 44, 99, 100, 111, 115

ear 34
earth14, 15, 16, 21, 86, 90, 91, 94, 97, 100, 109, 114, 124, 130, 159, 168, 173
earth energy 14, 21, 86, 90, 91, 94, 97, 100, 109, 130
eating disorders 40
Eilat Stone 72
Elestial 74, 139
Emerald 74, 75
emotional scars 14
endurance 17
Enstatite 68
Epidote 76
exhaustion. 17, 40, 41, 60, 79, 132
expression .25, 28, 33, 55, 72, 92, 100, 102, 138
eye42, 50, 51, 64, 93, 102, 175, 182
eyes 34, 35, 138, 188
fear14, 23, 51, 52, 57, 103, 117, 120, 129, 131, 143, 144, 163, 184
feet 81, 125, 155
feng shui 5, 10, 36, 133
fever .21, 52, 73, 103, 144, 160, 168
fidelity 74, 90, 118
fire 16, 123
flexibility ...22, 54, 56, 67, 155
Flint 77, 83
Fluorite 77, 78
friendliness 78
Fuchsite 78
gall bladder 50
Garnet 79

gazing .. 10, 29, 50, 52, 75, 88, 91, 101, 102, 114, 123, 124, 128, 130, 132, 139, 140, 147, 152, 154, 157, 162, 164, 177, 184

Gem Silica 54, 159

generosity56, 90, 118, 143

gentle 15

Geodes 81

glaucoma 68

goal oriented 22

goddess 115

Gold 40, 46, 81, 82, 133

Goldstone 82

good energy 29, 31, 59, 66, 76, 114, 123, 145, 160, 186

good luck .. 27, 35, 41, 151, 167

Granite 83

grounding 14, 15, 17, 21, 24, 27, 52, 78, 83, 84, 94, 96, 100, 105, 109, 114, 120, 121, 124, 133, 137, 151, 152, 160, 163, 168, 172, 175, 180, 186

growths 15

hair . 83, 87, 134, 140, 166

Hawk's Eye 84

headache 21, 170

healing stone 22, 136, 138

Heals 15

heart 20, 29, 33, 35, 37, 40, 41, 46, 49, 50, 54, 56, 59, 62, 65, 66, 69, 72, 75, 77, 86, 87, 88, 90, 99, 100, 103, 106, 114, 116, 118, 120, 122, 127, 128, 129, 132, 138, 140, 143, 144, 145, 146, 148, 155, 157, 159, 161, 170, 172, 177, 182, 189

Heart ... 15, 19, 69, 81, 116, 133, 169, 181, 184

heat 15, 54

Hematite 84

Herkimer Diamonds .. 85, 137

Hiddenite 86

honesty 41, 75, 81

Howlite 87

hunger 28, 117, 124

hypertension 28

imagination ... 61, 125, 182

immune system19, 34, 41, 57, 60, 90, 94, 102, 106, 113, 118, 127, 138, 140, 157, 162, 164, 179, 186

increased circulation 15

inner conviction 17

insomnia ... 22, 49, 51, 75, 78, 101, 102, 117, 143, 164, 178, 188

intestines .. 40, 58, 59, 96, 134

intuition 17, 31, 33, 61, 74, 101, 115, 151, 184

Iolite 88

Ivory 88

Jade 90, 91, 92, 93

Jasper 94, 95, 96, 137

Jet 97, 161

joints 44, 59, 71

joy 19, 66, 93, 148

kidneys 14, 40, 42, 44, 46, 47, 58, 79, 85, 118

knowledge 25, 61, 147

Kundalini Quartz 98

kundilini 157

Kunzite 98
Kyanite 100
Labradorite 101
Lapis Lazuli 101
Larimar 102
leadership 148, 161
Lepidolite 104
listlessness ... 40, 170, 177
liver14, 40, 42, 44, 47, 58,
    95, 96, 106, 127, 145,
    171, 178
Lodestone 104
loss .. 21, 27, 28, 102, 103,
    143
love 13, 19, 35, 40, 48, 54,
    57, 59, 69, 74, 87, 90,
    99, 104, 123, 143, 144,
    146, 148
love spells 13
lunar 60, 127, 136, 139
lungs... 34, 60, 69, 70, 81,
    94, 99, 106, 116, 134,
    157, 189
lymph nodes.. 34, 75, 162,
    164, 171
magnet 21, 25, 31, 104,
    141, 167
Malachite 106, 107
Marascite 109
Marble 111
massage 19, 142
meditation4, 5, 10, 14, 15,
    17, 24, 28, 29, 31, 33,
    34, 35, 38, 42, 46, 48,
    50, 52, 54, 57, 61, 65,
    66, 69, 72, 75, 78, 81,
    84, 85, 88, 90, 95, 98,
    100, 101, 106, 111, 115,
    120, 125, 128, 130, 131,
    132, 134, 136, 138, 140,

143, 144, 146, 147, 149,
    151, 152, 154, 155, 157,
    161, 162, 163, 167, 173,
    180, 182, 184
memory 21, 22, 56, 86,
    109, 160
metabolism 60, 62, 65,
    96, 145, 164, 171, 186
Meteorite 111
Mochi Balls 112
Moldavite 114
moonlight 9
Moonstone ... 114, 117, 161
Morganite 115
Mother of Pearl 117
mouth 28, 34, 72
muscle cramps 46
Muscovite 117
nausea 40
negative energy . 7, 20, 21,
    24, 36, 42, 57, 75, 97,
    99, 106, 108, 109, 127,
    141, 167, 179
negativity... 13, 45, 52, 57,
    122, 149, 181
neglect 69, 145
Nephrite 118
nerves .. 19, 34, 35, 48, 62,
    64, 81
nervous system21, 37, 40,
    49, 61, 62, 64, 66, 82,
    91, 96, 102, 118, 151,
    160, 178
nose 34
Obsidian 120, 121, 122,
    123, 124
Onyx 124, 125, 137, 154
Opal 125, 126
openness ... 29, 36, 48, 51,
    62, 70, 74

optimism.......... 52, 56, 77

pain 14, 15, 27, 42, 46, 54, 72, 103, 105, 106, 170, 171, 188

pancreas46, 105, 107, 171, 178, 189

past lives.... 21, 23, 25, 37, 39, 44, 65, 66, 79, 99, 129, 132, 162, 173, 182

patience.....28, 54, 59, 74, 79, 87, 116

peace ... 14, 32, 41, 54, 64, 72, 74, 88, 90, 111, 118, 128, 130

Pearl 125, 127, 128

Pecos Diamonds.........128

Peridot........................129

Petalite 129

Petrified Wood.......... 130

Phenacite.................... 131

phlegmatic................... 43

pituitary gland.....160, 171

Platinum.....................132

power . 20, 56, 65, 74, 85, 95, 101, 107, 109, 138, 148

powerful.....14, 19, 30, 31, 44, 52, 53, 68, 69, 72, 81, 83, 86, 90, 92, 98, 100, 111, 112, 116, 124, 129, 131, 160, 167, 177, 178

practicality 52

pregnant...................... 37

Prehnite......................132

prosperity. 20, 24, 27, 35, 41, 74, 82, 86, 95, 134, 167

protection... 13, 16, 18, 27, 33, 94, 95, 96, 111, 121, 133, 137, 149, 151, 167, 168, 178

psychic 22, 33, 37, 43, 44, 51, 52, 59, 63, 74, 75, 81, 83, 84, 86, 88, 102, 106, 115, 117, 122, 125, 130, 131, 132, 134, 136, 138, 143, 149, 152, 160, 163, 170

Pyrite................. 133, 134

Quartz ..85, 136, 137, 138, 139, 140, 141, 143, 149, 162, 180, 186

quit smoking 15

rage............................ 23

Reduces tension 14

reiki 4, 5, 10, 54, 133, 136, 146, 152, 163

respiratory systems.....19, 130, 134

rheumatism...59, 78, 130, 171

Rhodochrosite............144

Rhodonite 146

Rhyolite.....................147

ritual.......................14, 66

rituals ... 13, 14, 15, 21, 44, 66, 112

Root........... 14, 17, 27, 140

Ruby............148, 166, 167

sadness........................ 27

Sapphire..............151, 152

Sard.............152, 153, 154

Sardonyx 137, 154

sclerosis.................... 130

selection 4, 5

Selenite......................154

self confidence 17, 21

self control 15, 111

self esteem.... 19, 101, 116, 138, 145
self-esteem 16, 85, 123
Serpentine 157
sex 22, 56, 58, 61, 124
sexual desire 36
sexual energy 16, 61
sharing 25
Shiva Lingham 159
Silver 159, 160
singers 20, 62
sinus 37, 164, 171
skeletal structure 15
skin 15, 37, 59, 64, 68, 69, 75, 87, 93, 96, 104, 111, 128, 134, 140, 144, 151, 166, 171, 184
sleep apnea 22, 117
smell 48, 162
Smithsonite 161
smog 15
smoke 15, 161
Snowflake 123
sober 22, 88, 148
Sodalite 163
solar plexus 20, 21, 40, 42, 60, 70, 72, 81, 106, 109, 129, 145, 175, 176, 178, 182
soothes 20, 44, 48, 59, 60, 62, 107
Spectrolite 101
spine.... 21, 40, 61, 67, 85, 98, 155, 157
Spinel 166
spirits 25, 29, 34, 53
spiritual faith 20
spiritual growth 40
spiritual healing 40, 59

spleen .. 14, 19, 37, 42, 46, 50, 65, 77, 85, 96, 107, 186, 189
stability 14, 17, 85
stamina 20, 65, 76, 90, 118, 148, 178
Staurolite 167
Stichtite 169
Stilbite 169
stomach14, 21, 39, 40, 59, 96, 106, 134, 172, 175, 189
stress 15, 19, 22, 33, 35, 39, 47, 62, 72, 87, 92, 99, 103, 104, 115, 117, 121, 125, 143, 153, 160, 166, 168, 170, 179, 182, 184
Sugilite 170
Sulphur 171
sunlight 9, 42, 60, 104, 181
Sunstone 172
talismans 13, 127
Tanzanite 173
taste buds 34
teeth ... 34, 71, 77, 87, 125, 146
Tektite 173
testicles 68
third eye 17, 48, 50, 56, 61, 63, 77, 79, 84, 85, 92, 99, 100, 101, 103, 104, 106, 114, 131, 155, 170
throat...20, 25, 28, 31, 33, 37, 40, 48, 54, 60, 62, 92, 100, 102, 116, 122, 138, 151, 161, 163, 173, 181

thyroid.25, 28, 37, 54, 62, 107, 151, 164

Tiger's Eye...........137, 175

tissues......................... 25

Topaz.......................... 177

Tourmaline. 178, 179, 180

travel ...25, 29, 33, 44, 81, 84, 85, 88, 96, 112, 120, 122, 131, 132, 136, 184

trust..20, 27, 99, 116, 145, 169, 189

Turquoise........... 161, 180

ulcers...... 40, 54, 134, 175

Ulexite........................182

Unakite.......................182

uncertainty...................15

Variscite 184

vibrations .7, 9, 17, 19, 20, 22, 24, 25, 27, 29, 31, 43, 51, 56, 59, 66, 83, 86, 93, 102, 111, 114, 120, 123, 124, 129, 141, 149, 152, 155, 162, 168, 173, 181

visualization... 61, 85, 88, 96, 125, 177

waste elimination.. 25, 58

water ... 9, 33, 42, 46, 101, 103, 104, 114, 115, 120, 121, 122, 125, 127, 133, 136, 139, 159, 178, 182

wealth.....31, 90, 118, 129, 148, 177

weight control 25

wisdom....56, 90, 118, 151

wounds15, 18, 35, 153, 171

writers 20

Wulfenite................... 186

yang.....35, 65, 72, 73, 82, 90, 96, 109, 118, 124, 130, 149, 174, 176

yin 109, 114, 159, 174, 176

ying....35, 72, 73, 90, 103, 104, 125, 130

yoga...4, 24, 98, 133, 146, 155, 157, 180, 184

Zebra Stone............... 188

Zircon........................ 188

Zoisite................188, 189

Made in the USA
Monee, IL
30 September 2023

43730861R00085